My Journey
Cart *to* Aeroplane

LIFE AS A PROFESSIONAL BANKER

BIKER SINGH MANN

Copyright © Biker Singh Mann 2024
All Rights Reserved.

ISBN 979-8-89446-681-1

This book has been published with all efforts taken to make the material error-free after the consent of the author. However, the author and the publisher do not assume and hereby disclaim any liability to any party for any loss, damage, or disruption caused by errors or omissions, whether such errors or omissions result from negligence, accident, or any other cause.

While every effort has been made to avoid any mistake or omission, this publication is being sold on the condition and understanding that neither the author nor the publishers or printers would be liable in any manner to any person by reason of any mistake or omission in this publication or for any action taken or omitted to be taken or advice rendered or accepted on the basis of this work. For any defect in printing or binding the publishers will be liable only to replace the defective copy by another copy of this work then available.

Dedicated in the memory of my great teacher, Sh Rawal Singh, who always devoted his life for the upliftment of the poor in the society by way of education. Education is most powerful weapon for the improving the life of people on the earth.

This book is also dedicated to my mother and father whose contribution in life cannot be measured or explained by any words.

CONTENTS

MY JOURNEY
CART TO AEROPLANE
Biker Singh Mann

FOREWORD

First of all, let me congratulate Shri. B S Mann, Chief General Manager (retired), Punjab National Bank for taking the initiative to write a book titled "CART TO AEROPLANE", which essentially captures his journey from a village boy with hardships to reach at the senior management position in a public sector bank. This book is written at a time when a need was felt to have some guidance to the present and future generation on how to be a successful leader, banker and how to navigate against all odds.

The book provides a perspective which is unique and enriching. Behind each story lies an element of determination, fighting instinct, decisions, confidence and conviction. It provides practical lessons and could be useful for present and future generations.

The stories and incidents of handling of various issues at several stages in his career throw light on how to put institution's interest first and at the same time build the personal career by gaining experience in handling unexpected challenges. The book also throws light on several aspects of leadership qualities especially during uncertain times.

The author who was not from a privileged background, went on to become a successful banker by not compromising on his faith, confidence and principles while dealing with challenges. He worked with sincerity and availed the first available opportunity of any kind to serve the organisation. Right from his school days to become a banker and subsequently building his career in banking, Shri. Mann had worked with focus and determination coupled with dedication and meticulous planning to take advantage of the opportunities to reach at the leadership roles. How opportunities came to him and how these were utilized are all narrated in this book. Hence, this book is in a way a guidance notes for today's leaders, career bankers and students who wish to join banking sector.

World Trade Centre Complex, Centre 1, 6th Floor, Cuffe Parade, Mumbai - 400 005. • Tel: 022 2217 4040 / 69234040 • Website: www.iba.org.in

Human beings are mortal. However, his ideas captured in the form of a book are immortal. When someone reads this book written by Shri Mann, they will be enriched with good ideas on dealing with difficult situations. At times, conventional methods may not suffice, you may have to think out of the box to tackle a unique situation. Through various chapters of the book, the author has taken pains to share his experiences and through these real-life examples have provided several tools to deal with the challenges with ease.

The author has beautifully summarized certain tips which are essentially drawn from his experiences which could be useful to new generation bankers. These are as follows:

- ✓ If interest is there, no job is impossible
- ✓ Attend meetings with seniors after thorough preparation and with confidence and with right attitude.
- ✓ Extend full co-operation to auditors and inspectors as they have to do their job.
- ✓ Approach customers with cool mind and without any ego. Please understand you are there because of the customers.
- ✓ Closing of audit reports is very important in the career of a banker.

Happy Reading.

Date: 18th June 2024
Location: Mumbai

Sunil Mehta
Chief Executive
Indian Banks' Association

INTRODUCTION

This book is being written and released when the banking industry grapples with unique human resources challenges. With a younger workforce, there is a need for more exposure and experience in handling banking, coupled with the increasing age-related responsibilities they have to take on. The experiences I share in this book, despite the operational changes in banking, are not just relevant but also reassuring and confidence-boosting from a management perspective and for conducting business in the changing landscape of the banking industry. They are a testament that these challenges are not insurmountable, and success is within reach with the right strategies and mindset.

In this book, I have shared various experiences handling multiple banking issues and strategies to increase the business while working as branch head, circle head, zonal manager, and head office assignments. While writing the book, I was uncertain which memories were relevant. My childhood is precious to me, but would it interest anyone? You may wonder about the tribulations and triumphs of a small village boy—the strained circumstances at home and his family background. However, I got great help from my first teacher, who imparted my primary education; otherwise, I may be unable to reach where I am. In college, I overcame difficulties, faced challenges from the front, and gave a befitting reply to the teasers. With a clear mind, I will do or die fighting how I availed the opportunities as and when available without compromising my ethics. This journey, filled with ups and downs, has shaped me into the professional I am today, and I hope it inspires you to overcome your challenges and strive for success.

I hope this story is an account not just of my triumphs and tribulations but also of the successes and setbacks of a rural boy who fought to establish himself. By inspiring this story, I hope many may find the way.

GOD creates each creature on this beautiful planet to fulfill a particular role. Whatever I have achieved in life is through His help and expression of His will. He showered His grace upon me through some outstanding teachers, colleagues, and parents' bosses, and when I pay my tributes to these acceptable persons, I merely praise His glory.

I believe everyone struggles to achieve something in life. Without struggle, it isn't significant if you have achieved anything. The things you have achieved with struggle give you more satisfaction and happiness—everyone who has achieved something on his footing, hard work, and sincerity achieved values for him. There is no measurement to measure the achievements, big or small, etc.; it differs from person to person. I think a person's satisfaction, happiness, and contentment measure the level of achievements. One achievement may not be of much value for one, while for others, it may be of great value. Whatever I have achieved, I am delighted, happy, and content. Further, this was not my target whatsoever I achieved. I have no target in my career, but I remained satisfied, happy, and contended on every stage of the ladder. From my start of education to my retirement, even today. I was pleased and confident that whatever I achieved was on my footing, hard work, and sincerity.

We are all born with a divine fire in us. Our efforts should be to give wings to this fire and fill the world with the glow of its goodness.

This book is also a submission of thanks to my teachers, neighbors, parents, wife, colleagues, and preceptors I have been fortunate to have had both as students and in my professional life.

Above all, I am very thankful to Sh AK Roy Choudhary, DGM, retired PNB; this book would not have been presented without his guidance and support.

CHAPTER 1

EDUCATION

INTRODUCTION

Everyone in life struggles to achieve something. Without struggles, it isn't significant if you have achieved anything. The things you have achieved with struggles give you endless satisfaction and happiness. Everyone who has achieved something through his efforts, hard work, and sincerity is of great value to him. There is no defined yardstick by which one can measure achievements, whether small or big, as they differ from person to person. In my opinion, a person's level of satisfaction, happiness, and contentment can be a reasonable way to measure their level of achievement. Also, it is possible that one achievement may not be of much value for one person, while for others, it may have great value. Whatever I have achieved, I am satisfied, happy, and content. Further, this was not the target I had achieved, and the fact remains that I had no planned target in my career. I always did my best at every stage of the ladder, which my bank allowed me to work on. From the start of my education to my retirement, I am happy and satisfied that whatever I have achieved was based on my efforts, hard work, sincerity, and, of course, because of my elders' and seniors' support and guidance. The story of my struggles, efforts, and achievements and the contribution of several people in this journey, which I feel worth sharing with others, is the theme of my book, which I am sure will inspire many.

FAMILY AND EDUCATION

I retired as Chief General Manager from Punjab National Bank on 31st March 2022, after completing 38 years and seven months of service in the bank from the Delhi corporate Head Office. I joined as a clerk in the bank on 26th August 1983, soon after I had completed my B. Com degree. When someone joins any job nowadays, he always knows about future opportunities. Still, in those days, I got the job and was very much satisfied as my only mission was to get a good job, and then I had no idea about the future opportunities in the job. The key reason was that more than any career opportunities in the job, I was focused on getting the job because of the economic condition of my family. During those days, I was not alone, that my financial position required a job, but almost all of that generation required some job or work to support their respective families.

START OF EDUCATION

I still vividly remember those days when I was about 5 /6 years old. One evening, when I was sitting with my father, a marginal farmer, two or three people from our neighbourhood came to our house, asked my name, and enquired whether I wanted to attend school. On giving consent to my father, they requested my father to send me to Dharamshala (a community centre) of the village the next day as one teacher who had settled in the town after retirement had started the school in Dharamshala to give free education to the children of the village.

So, I started going to Dharmshala (community centre) for education the next day. I continued there for 2/3 years; during that period, I learned the counting and basics of the Punjabi language and many other things that were required to be taught in primary education. My father had, unfortunately, no opportunity to undergo any schooling, and even my entire family, including my uncles, my father's uncles, and forefathers, had no education due to financial conditions besides the lack of facilities for education in such remote villages.

I was the first to get the opportunity for formal education in my family. My father was a very humble and straightforward person engaged in agriculture, with the status of a marginal farmer with no other source of income. I was the eldest of 5 siblings. Although I got the education because of the family of Shri Rawal Singh (the retired teacher who started school in village Dharmshala), all of my brothers and sisters could not get the opportunity for formal education except one sister who passed 8th class only.

One day, after six months of my going to school in Dharmshala, the teacher called my father along with me at his residence in the evening and said briefly, '**eh Munda school aye ga Harroj, app fees and books de skate Ho Jan Nain koi gal Nain main khud Karenga parbandh but eh parega** (this boy should come to school every day. If you could not bear the cost of books and fees no issue, I would manage but I would ensure he gets the education). I also have vivid memories of that conversation, and I was happy. Up to the class of 5th, I was always with him in two or three private schools, where he joined as a teacher after retirement. Shri Rawal Singh had four sons and three daughters, all educated and employed in due course. The entire family was taking care of my education. When I was in 6th class, he left his private job, but before that, he had managed my admission to a recognized school (Khalsa High School Mansa). But daily in the evening, I visited him at his house for guidance. One day, he called his grown-up children and put the responsibility of my education on their shoulders. When I was in class 8th, Shri Rawal Singh had unfortunately passed away. His two elder sons are Shri Inderjit Singh and Shri Paramjit Singh Gill. Shri Paramjit Singh Gill retired as IG of Punjab Police later. On the passing away of Shri Rawal Singh, I felt unfortunate and was worried about what would happen to my education now. Thankfully, the family supported me with their guidance, and I passed the 10th class, missing the first division by a few marks then. In villages at that time, it was thought that boys would become careless, astray towards their families if they go to college. As such, my father and grandmother were not interested in sending me to college for further education. The other reason was financial reasons. With the advice of my teacher's family and some other villagers (my neighbour, a primary teacher, Sh Balbir Singh), my father agreed to my admission to 10+1 in a school. I had opted for arts subjects with Economics, cleared 10+1 with good marks, and secured first division in Economics and English. I also had a good ranking in class.

PASSING OF B.COM

After seeing my excellent result of 10+1 and with the guidance of my teachers' family and neighbours, my father agreed to send me to college for further education. As per the guidance of my teacher's son, I filled up the admission form for admission to BA part 1 as an art student. However, before submitting it, I got the form checked by Sh Paramjit Singh Gill. While sitting on the wood log in the village in the evening, he checked my form but changed the admission form from B. A part 1 to B. Com part

1. At that time, the word B. Com was new to me. But he gave me some ideas about the B. Com course and assured me of all the help. Accordingly, I took the admission in B. Com course. **Before going to college, my father had advised me one thing: as he had no formal education, wasn't aware of the studies I was going to pursue, and didn't know anything about college education, it would be my responsibility to do justice to the faith reposed by him and others in me. He further added that he would pay fees and arrange to purchase books out of his hard-earned money.** Now, it was my responsibility to meet their expectations and study well. These words had put more responsibility on me.

There were 40 students in the class, and there were only three of us, along with two of my friends, who had a background in the village and had studied only art subjects. All the other students had done 10+1 in commerce, and naturally, they had an edge over us. There used to be ragging on us in college. One of them used the language "OHH JATTO, (sons of farmers and from villages) commerce pass 'Karna aap Ke bas main Nain hi app arts karo' (oh farmers sons you cannot pass commerce, take admission in arts) we were not able to understand the commerce subjects and the double entry system of bookkeeping, and others were ragging on us and pressure was on us that if we failed, our parents would not allow us to continue further studies and our future would be ruined. And if we go back to art classes, they will create more problems for us. We were standing at a crossroads. Now, the real struggle had started. We decided **to die fighting and accept the challenge of studying B. Com but would not surrender.** This was the pledge taken by us. Our mission was to pursue B. Com; thus, an essential phase of the journey started.

I took the challenge and thought that only hard work and belief in God could help me overcome the problem, so I planned my further studies accordingly. There were five subjects in the syllabus, and in order of priority, I had given the time for each subject to study in a day. Whatever chapter to be taught by the professor, I used to prepare the same one day before. In the evening, I would revise the same chapter from other books as I had started consulting three books on each subject. This began in September. Out of 24 hours, I put around 14 hours in a day for my studies. After one month, I gained some confidence. The first in-house exam started in December, and how I solved the papers gave me confidence that I would not fail. But the day the professor announced the result to all students in the class except me, and obviously, I was worried. Then he announced that there was a hidden 'Rustam' in the class and that I was on top of the list in class. This was sufficient to shut the mouths of many. From that date, the professor allotted me the first seat in the class instead of the last seat. When I had to sit in the first seat, it put more pressure on me to perform and inspired me to continue to do well.

The annual exams were held in April. After being free from continuous study for the past eight months, I was free, and harvesting season started. I contributed to the family by harvesting wheat, Sarson, and Channa crops. It was physical labour of almost one and a half months. One day, after being free from the farming activity, along with my classmates, I went to college to deposit the library books I had borrowed. One of my other classmates also joined us when we were having tea on the lawn. His close relative was working at the university, and on many occasions, he had shared much news about the university in advance, which used to be always true. He started to deliberate on exam results and told me that he had come from university and the result of our class B. Com part 1 is almost ready, which is terrible for our college; many students have failed. He informed my other friends and me that we had failed in three papers and that the result was that we failed. All our hopes were dashed to the ground; darkness was before our eyes. However, we consoled ourselves and came back to home. We had not said anything to anyone, but inside, there was uneasiness about thinking about the future. I wondered how I could be failing after putting in a lot of hard work and the confidence I gained by solving the papers.

After 20 days, the results were declared in the newspaper one morning. When I went through the results, I again found myself at the top of the list in the class, and my other friend cleared the exam with good marks. Now you can imagine how the 20 days in my life would have passed, and I can never forget those distressed days. At that time, I thought life was swinging between ruins and success. But it was a matter of great sorrow for me that my classmate, who had gone to university and shared the false news about the result, had failed. He was not able to clear the B.Com.

My success and top of the list in the class made my head high among my professors and classmates.

WHEN YOU PUT IN HARD WORK, DETERMINATION, AND ACCEPT THE CHALLENGE, YOU WILL NEVER FAIL. IF YOU HAVE TO DIE, DIE FIGHTING NOT BEFORE THAT.

After completing B. Com Part 1, I joined the next class. By that time, I had established myself among my professors, friends, and in college.

I took admission in B. Com part II. One of the subjects was statistics, but before the start of classes, my friend Amrik Singh and I covered the entire syllabus of statistics with the guidance of Sh Paramjit Singh Gill, the son of Sh Rawal Singh, my teacher. In those days, he prepared for Punjab Civil Services; later, he cleared the same and was selected as DSP in Punjab police. Our efforts to cover the syllabus in this way gave us a good amount of confidence and an edge over the other classmates. However, due to some complacency developed in me, I was placed second in the class in the results. I was unhappy with myself, and I learned so many lessons. From this result, I became more severe about B. Com III. I also thought about the shortcomings and the way to overcome them. In the final year, I put in serious effort and burnt the midnight oil, and as a result, I was again placed at the top of the list in college, beating all odds.

In one of the B. Com final papers, the subject was cost accounting, and the question paper standard was very high, beyond the expectations of the professor and students. Half of the class left the exam centre when the paper was distributed, but I did not. What I did was, with patience and presence of mind, solved the paper by reading word by word, and I got the highest marks on this paper, which gave me an edge over my competitors.

I want to pay particular gratitude to my parents, who put everything of theirs into my education. I do not know how they managed all my expenses for this higher education. My mother constantly supported me, and it goes beyond this monetary one. When I used to study at night on cold nights, she would get up at 11 pm and prepare a cup of tea for me on those bitter cold nights by lighting a fire, which used to take 15 minutes. Then, I used to take a nap to re-energize myself. And I continue to study by 2 am. This would happen almost five days a week. Had my mother not put in these efforts, I might not have been successful, and thus, my special gratitude to my mother. Otherwise also, a person never forgets their mother's contribution, who is God for all of us. I have no words here to write about mothers' gratitude in life.

Our house had no electricity connection, and I used to study with the help of an oil lamp. When I was in class 10th, one of our neighbours extended one electric bulb to our house only for my studies. So, one bulb hung on our side of the wall by a wire extending from their house. I am also thankful to the family for their support.

Take Aways

- **Always accept the challenge; it is better to die fighting than to surrender.**
- **You will never fail when you put in hard work and determination and accept the challenge.**

CHAPTER 2

ENTRY IN BANK

SELECTION IN BANK

I was also a basketball player both at the school level and at the college level as I was concentrating more on my studies; as such, I was not able to give much time for sports. Even then, I played up to the district level at the school level, and our team was runners-up at the district level. In college, I played only at the zone level. Our team usually played basketball after 5 pm daily on college grounds. We were 11-12 players, and a good game was played by two teams of 5 each. Many of my fellow players have played at the national level, and I am very proud of them, namely Pardeep Kumar, Daljit, and Inderjit.

One day, it so happened that two or three players had gone on leave, and we could not have a complete game, so when they joined, all were rebuking them for why they had gone on leave. Then, Vinod Kumar, a senior at B. Com, told me that he had to appear for the bank's recruitment exam. This matter immediately struck me, and I called him separately and requested him to guide me about the bank's exam. Before that, I did not know anything about recruitment in the bank. Thanks to my friend Shri Vinod Kumar, who later joined the Oriental Bank of Commerce and retired as

Chief Manager, I, too, became a banker. He not only guided me but also, when the subsequent vacancies were advertised, got a form and IPO (Indian postal order) of Rs. 20 for me. He also handed over the study material for the exam, which he had used for his preparations. Because of the guidance of Shri Vinod Kumar, I got the inspiration and prepared for the bank clerical exam.

The test was on date 20 June 1982 at 9 AM in Ludhiana. It was the month of May, and our family, along with me, were busy in Rabi crop harvesting. I was, as usual, contributing a lot to the same, but on the other hand, I had to appear in the competition exam. Only one and half month period was available for preparation. I stopped giving a helping hand for rabi crop harvesting and started the preparation for the exam. My father and other family members were unhappy with this decision and were not even talking to me. However, I avoided getting into any arguments with them and instead concentrated on the preparation of the test.

I got my Hall admission card with roll number by post, and I am still holding that Hall card with roll number LD2617104. The exam centre was Ludhiana. My native town was Mansa, and no bus service was available early in the morning to reach Ludhiana on time, but it was available from Bathinda. So, I and my other friends reached Bathinda a day before and stayed at a relative's house. The next morning, I boarded a bus for Ludhiana at 4.30 a.m. and confidently took the exam. However, I did not know whether I would qualify then, as it was a new experience. The result was declared in the local newspaper on 26th Feb 1983. One of my close friends came to my house in the evening to inform me that I had qualified for the exam. The result was declared in a newspaper, and no other source was available to confirm the result. The interview was held on 6th April 1983 at Ludhiana, and the final selection result was declared on 13th June 1983. Again, on the final selection, one of my close friends told me about my selection, and the result was declared in the local newspaper.

Before that, when I had to appear for an interview, there were so many discouraging talks in the village about clearing interviews; as per prevailing rumours in the villages, one would clear the interview who had some recommendations or by greasing the palm of officials, and I had no such recommendations and had no money. But as per my ideals, I would not have opted for any of these. However, my father was quite depressed by listening to such baseless rumours. Still, I was confident that, with a qualification as a B. Com with first division, I would be selected for the clerk post. I was also thinking that if I had not been selected, then I would have no sorrow as I would have considered it a loss to the bank (this was wishful thinking)

JOINING THE BANK

When the result was declared, I received another letter from BSRB informing me that I had been allocated to PNB. I got the appointment letter by post on 13th August 1983 from Regional Office Firozpur of PNB, and the station where I had to join was Sardulgarh, just 40 km from Mansa. On 25th August 1983, after completing the joining formalities, I reached the branch to join. Still, I was not allowed to join because my medical certificate issued by the CMO did not have the details of all medical tests done. I requested the Branch Manager that the CMO issue a certificate on these lines only and all relevant records be for their record, but The Manager was not ready to listen. I was advised to get all the details.

When this news reached my village, the market of rumours was so hot that you had to pay money to join. Again, I contested the views of villagers and my father, who was unaware of things and did not know anything about this. My father approached a political person for help, but their views were again not as I thought, so we ignored their advice. My father then approached our commission agent (the commission agent helps the farmers to sell their crops and also arranges money for the needs of the farmer's family) with whom we have been dealing for the last 50 years, and luckily, the Manager was his neighbour. The commission agent asked me to request the Manager to allow me to join, and if any other papers were required, I would be permitted to produce them later on. When we met the Manager the following day, it came to our notice that the brother of the Manager was very well known to my father, so all hurdles were cleared. It was a great relief for me and my father.

Ultimately, I joined the bank on 26 August 1983, and when I was allowed to sit in the branch at that moment, my feelings and happiness were beyond words. That was the first day when I thought that whatever was required in life, God had given me, and I did not have any other desire before God. Other desires were supplementary to that.

Take Aways

- **Keep your faith, confidence, and ideals intact. Any rumours should not let this down.**
- **When you are true to your ideals, God always helps you.**

CHAPTER 3

TRANSFER TO MANSA BRANCH

PASSING CAIIB AND M.COM

After working for 15 months there, on request, I was transferred to branch Mansa, my home town, where I worked from 17th December 1984 to 15th July 1989 in the clerical cadre. Most of the time, I worked on loan seats and learned all types of banking in the branch as I was putting all my dedication to learning and work.

In life, I always think about small goals and follow them. I never think of huge goals to avoid frustration and have always succeeded. After joining the bank, I never thought about any other job but concentrated on my present job and thinking about how to achieve further success. So, I fixed two goals. The first is to clear the Certified Associate Exam, i.e., CAIIB, which is very important in every banker's career for banking law and other relevant knowledge. It was also helpful to get the extra increments and marks in promotion processes to place you ahead of others. So, I started to prepare for this exam and did M. Com by correspondence. I completed both in two years. There were 14 clerks in the branch, and I was the junior most. When I cleared both exams, I was next to senior most in seniority in the branch.

So, I always worked in senior positions in leave gap arrangements. Taking my lead, some other staff members also started preparing for the CAIIB exam, and 2/3 cleared the same.

PENSION PAYMENTS

While working in the clerical cadre as the second senior, I worked on the Teller payments seat. There were about 600 pensioners who came to the branch in the first 7/8 days of the month to draw the pension. Most of them were defence pensioners, so, continuously working on the seat, at least 80% of pensioners became well-known faces to me. I adopted a practice that up to the payment of Rs1000 (this amount was equal to my one-month salary at that time, and about 80% of pensioners had pensions less than this amount), there was no need to tally the signature and a rush of about 140 payments per day cleared by 1 pm, all pensioners were very happy and it contributed a lot for customer services. As and when any day someone else was sitting on that seat, there was always commotion, and pensioners always insisted that I should be called to work on that seat. Although with this practice, our customers were pleased, my colleagues were annoyed with me for following the practice of not verifying the signature and making payments. However, I was always happy to provide good customer service by taking calculated risks, which was the need of the hour.

But one day, it happened that there was an excess payment made to one pensioner. It came to my knowledge when I was tallying the cash that out of 140 payments, I focussed on all, but my doubt was on one pensioner. During lunchtime, I went directly to his home and rang the bell. The same pensioner came out with an excess amount in his hand and told me that he was about to come to the bank to refund it, as it had come to his notice when he reached home. He also said that you need not worry about payments. No one will keep your money as your service toward defence pensioners was excellent, and all were very happy.

LEARNING LOAN PORTFOLIO

In the branch, my allocated seat was as a loans clerk. I learned a lot about agriculture loans and industry loans. At that time, a lot of agriculture machinery loans were disbursed. Every loan was processed by the Agriculture Officer and sanctioned by the Manager. My role was to execute the documents and open the account. While going through the files, I always prepared parallel processing notes and compared them with the notes of AO. In this way, I learned about agriculture loans and how to calculate the share of shareholders in the joint ownership land record, and I also learned how to study the land revenue records. I even got the help of the father of one of my friends, who was working as Patwari.

With the guidance of the Branch Manager and due to my interest, I also started to learn about industry and business loans and learned a lot about these loans. Because of this, I developed the confidence to process and disburse loans up to Rs. 5 lakhs at that time.

CONFIDENCE

One day, the Manager and Assistant Manager went out for lunch. Around that time, a telephone call was received from another branch, which a clerical staff member attended, and the BM of another branch wanted to talk to the branch manager. The clerical staff replied that 1st man and the second man had gone out for lunch, then the BM of that branch requested him to hand over the telephone to the responsible staff and named me as he wanted some clarifications about loan matters. Therefore, I answered the phone and clarified the matter he asked for. This gave me much-needed confidence.

PROMOTION

The first time I qualified for the promotion exam for an officer was in 1988, on my first attempt, when I appeared for an interview. We were 74 candidates from Punjab, and out of 74, only 5 were CAIIB and M. Com, thus getting 25 marks out of 25 in education qualification as per promotion policy. We 5 were very confident about the promotion, keeping in view our marks, but when the result was declared, we all 5 were out. It wasn't very reassuring to see how it could happen. However, after seeing the results and inquiries, it was found that the bank cleared some reservation backlog. It was a statutory requirement, so we could not have any grudge. After a few months, another exam was announced, and I prepared very well for the same and appeared in the written exam. I qualified the same and appeared for an interview. In the interview, one of the members said, "Sardar ji, you have come a second time for this interview. Now, you need not come again for this interview." Luckily, the member was also a member of the interview committee for the first time. The interview result was declared on 28th June 1989. On those days, the communication was not so fast; the result came to my knowledge on 1st July through my branch manager, who came to my house at 9 pm in the night along with sweets to inform me and my parents that I had been promoted as an officer. I was very thankful to him for his support.

My parents, my in-laws, and I were pleased about my promotion, but when the posting order was received and the station for joining was about 200 km from Mansa's hometown, their mood changed. They said that they would have been happy if I had not accepted the promotion, but I was determined to go. The branch was Ferozeshah near Ferozepur, where I had to join. Earlier, I had never gone to Ferozepur, so first, I had to find some contacts to stay till I got a house on rent. My distant relatives were there because of their job, and my father contacted them from their village and got their address of Ferozepur. Then, one of our neighbours was a bus conductor in a government job, and his bus route was Mansa- Ferozepur, so he helped me reach Ferozeshah. I joined on promotion at Ferozeshah in Firozpur district on 17.07.1989.

Take Aways

- **You should be sincere towards your work and customers**
- **Learn about the first opportunity that is available to you.**

CHAPTER 4

WORKING AS AN OFFICER IN BANK

JOINING

I joined as an officer at branch Ferozeshah on 17.07.1989. The branch was in the border area of the Firozpur district. I remained there for over two years to complete my mandatorily rural service. The branch building was old and further, due to a disturbance in Punjab, all the windows of the branch were kept shut with iron sheets from a security point of view, and it was therefore challenging to work in summer. No cross ventilation, no light. We requested our manager to arrange a generator set as it was tough to work in such situations, and he, in turn, asked the Regional Manager to do the same. Our Regional Manager, Mr. K S Rajput, was so generous that he ordered the shift of the generator set used at his residence. We were all obliged.

PAYMENT OF SALARIES

The first problem in the branch was the payment of salaries of some state government employees. In the village, there was a substation of the Punjab State Electricity Board, and about 120 employees were getting salaries through our branch. Whenever a credit note was being received in the branch, the branch used to take one day to credit the salary in respective accounts, and the same was allowed to be withdrawn on the next day. As such, it used to take three days to pay the employees. They were very annoyed, and every month, employees in front of the branch organized a dharna. After joining, I started the practice of employees started getting a salary on the day of credit. As a result, there was no dharna, but our relationship with the employees improved, and that helped the bank garner a lot of business. I have always believed that 'every problem has a solution only if we have a positive attitude to our job.

During my stay in the branch, miscreants attempted to loot the branch twice. But thank God, there was no loss of any kind.

ATTEMPT OF ROBBERY IN THE BRANCH

One day on Saturday, there was no cash in the branch, and as the Manager was on leave, keeping in view the demand, I got sufficient cash arranged from the currency chest of the nearby branch. However, during the day, some cash was also received from customers, and cash brought from the currency chest remained unutilized. As usual, we closed the branch's cash after the banking hours. The next day was a holiday, so the miscreants took advantage and entered the branch through the bathroom window. Mostly in village branches, there was no strong room, and the cash safe was kept in an iron cage. The intruders cut the cage and reached the safe. They tried to open the lock with screwdrivers and other orthodox instruments but failed and ran away. Unfortunately, the police investigating officers asked why we had brought the cash on Saturday and started suspecting bank employees of their involvement. But with great difficulty, we were able to make them understand that it was a business call as per the requirement of the branch. As there was no loss to the bank, ultimately, he was satisfied with the contention of the bank.

VISIT OF REGIONAL MANAGER

One day in May, there was a rush of customers in the branch because of the crop season. Many customers were sitting in the branch, and the Manager was on leave. I was the only officer working and attending to the customers individually to their satisfaction. Suddenly, the Regional Manager came to visit the branch. After seeing so many customers sitting in the branch, he misunderstood that we, the staff, were not attending to the customers properly and started saying harsh words about the branch's working. At that time, one customer immediately stood up and praised the branch for its customer service. He told the Regional Manager that all the customers were satisfied and that the branch was doing well. The Regional Manager was satisfied and advised us to continue doing a good job, and left the office. I was afraid and told my manager everything when he returned the next day. In the next Manager Meeting, the Regional Manager expressed his appreciation for working in the branch.

FACING MILITANCY

The area was very disturbed because of the prevailing situation in Punjab then and because the branch was close to the border area. When we had to go to the field for recovery or field visits, one guard (being a local person) of the branch always used to accompany the concerned officer. Once, I and the guard were going for a field visit, and we were driving our scooter on the bank of canal. This was the only way to go to visit that area. The area was bushy, and 3/4 persons with guns appeared before us. We remained silent, and after some time, they allowed us to go, but while we were leaving, they told us that we were from the bank and they knew the guard as such, let us go otherwise, if the Manager (they thought I was Manager) was alone he could have been shot down. We had a fortunate escape that day.

The other incident relates to the same branch where there used to be always a call from Bandh at least one day a week on one issue or another in the area. On this type of call, all branches of banks and other offices used to remain closed for security reasons. Our branch was under regular inspection by a CA firm in Delhi. The auditor insisted on an inspection on a particular date, but there was a Bandh call that day. My manager and I had requested that we should not go to the branch that day for security reasons, but despite our best efforts, he insisted on going to the branch. We had no other option but to go to the branch on two scooters as there were two people. On Bandh's call, even bus service remained suspended. When we started from Ferozepur at 9.15 in the morning, the roads were deserted, and only our two vehicles were going on. I and the manager were under significant threat to our lives, yet we had to go. When we crossed halfway, three young men on the Bullet motorcycle came before us with guns. Again, we kept silent. Mostly, the men were from the local area and asked when there was a call for Bandh and why we were going to the branch. Then I explained to them that we would not open the branch but would take some files as these files were to be sent to Delhi tonight through these persons. Thank God, they allowed us. Seeing the above, both auditors insisted on returning immediately to Ferozepur without going to the branch. But I had requested them that we now go to the branch and would come back immediately. The auditor agreed with me, and we went to the branch and came back immediately. Those youths who had stopped on our way to the branch again met us and waved their hands. Now, auditors were very afraid, and they returned to Delhi, where the branch had to produce some records to complete the work.

ELECTION DUTY

Banking work was going smoothly, but the general law and order of the area were not good, and there was always fear. We did not know whether we would return in the evening. In this situation, elections were declared in Punjab. The militants announced a boycott call and said whoever would be involved in the process in any way would face consequences. Two three employees were shot dead in the state. There was total fear among all government employees because of election duty. I had also received a letter for election duty. While going through the letter, I found that I was appointed presiding officer, and the duty of our team was in a village polling booth. The entire logistic and security responsibility was with BSF. Our team started the journey from Ferozepur in a BSF truck and reached the village school. The instruction was that no eatables should be taken from the village and that everything, including security, would be managed by BSF and Punjab police. Three policemen were on our security duty, and the BSF truck had gone to another village with another team. The policemen called the village chowkidar and ordered him to arrange some stiff drinks. They consumed whiskey and also advised us to take some, adding that after taking this, there would be no fear. After taking a hard drink, they slept, leaving us without security and at the mercy of militants. Our team was shocked, and a firing was happening close to the village. We closed all the doors and sat in two rooms. Around 9 pm, a truck came at the gate; I could see through a small window that it was a BSF truck. They handed over the dinner box and asked if we had any problems. Then I told the commander about the behaviour of police on security, that they were all sleeping after drinking. He was also very annoyed and ordered two of his soldiers for our security; one was standing on the roof, and the other was at the gate. At 11 pm, three more soldiers were put on duty, and we breathed a sigh of relief. We were without security on the critical day in a village for about three hours. When I remember that moment, it was a very chilling one. Fortunately, everything went in the right way that evening.

WORKING IN THE REGIONAL OFFICE

In two years, the branch's business had doubled, deposits increased from Rs. 78 lacs to Rs. 140 lacs and advanced from Rs. 55 lacs to about Rs. 100 lacs. On completion of tenure of two years, I was transferred to the Regional Office on 3rd October 1991

Working in the regional office was a new experience for me. My job involved attending to several telephone calls, making calls to many branches, and putting up many notes for seniors, which I was not used to. As such, I had to learn much about this subject, work hard, and be willing to go the extra mile and to channel energy. I also worked in the HR department and thus learned a lot about working in the administrative office.

TRANSFER TO BATHINDA

After completing a stay of one year, I was transferred back to Bathinda Region, where I joined on 23.11.1992. Here, I was allotted again the duties of the HR department. I worked there till 10.05.1997. During my stay of about four and half years, I enjoyed a lot of my work. Being in the HR department, I extended a helping hand to the employees within the given rules regarding transfer and posting. I was also fortunate to receive much love and affection from all my colleagues. At that time, I was a scale one officer and had the opportunity to work under the guidance of two Regional Managers. The Regional Manager issued an office order that all files from my table would go directly to the Regional Manager's table, bypassing the Manager and Senior Manager. Once, the Regional Manager called me into his chamber and said, **''I have faith in your work. As such, this office order has been issued for you to send files directly to me''.** These words gave me a lot of confidence, and no file of my seat remained pending for disposal, while files of my other senior colleagues often remained pending. My working rule was to appraise the authorities about the bank's guidelines on the matter but take decisions as advised by authorities.

MERGER OF ENBI AND COURT CASES

In my career, I have always adhered to the policy of non-confrontation with juniors and seniors, working within the bank's norms. During my posting in the Regional Office, Bathinda, a significant event was the merger of the New Bank of India (NBI) with Punjab National Bank, which took place on 04.09.93. There were 13 branches of ENBI in our region. The first task was to post managers in these branches from PNB and obtain all the employees' consent to continue in PNB. The New Bank of India employee union significantly influenced NBI, but in PNB, it was not the case. Three leaders of the NBI union were posted in our region. The primary challenge before us was to manage these leaders. The other issue was that PNB unions also wanted to post these leaders to far-away places so they may be unable to dominate. In one of our branches, Sangrur Court Road, one leader directly threatened the Manager and started dictating to the Branch Manager about branch affairs. We, therefore, had to deal with this type of leadership, which required tactful handling for the smooth running of the branches. This strategic approach was crucial in maintaining the balance and ensuring the successful transition of the merger.

The Zonal Office exercised staff requirements at each station in each Region and each branch in consultation with Regional Offices. Based on total staff working and requirements per PNB norms, at BO Sangrur, the staff was declared surplus, including the leader dictating the Manager, and also at Bathinda. The list of surplus staff was prepared for posting out of station on seniority. The team at the Zonal Office advised us to issue transfer orders as per this exercise and for surplus staff to be posted within the region at a point of need. Accordingly, our region issued orders to post surplus staff. Still, the zonal office later sent a written communication stating that all surplus staff should be transferred to the Ferozepur region.

The verbal orders were taken back, and my position became awkward as the Regional Manager issued orders per my message. Still, the Zonal Office later sent a written letter from ZO was otherwise. There was a confrontation with higher-ups, and all the guns were pointed towards me. However, I had the confidence that I had correctly conveyed to the Regional Manager whatever was said to me by the Zonal Office staff. My close friends were also the officers who advised me to issue orders. When I enquired with them, they said that AGM (HR) had not agreed and that they were helpless. Our office managed to send some staff to Ferozepur, and my Regional Manager came forward for my rescue and told the AGM that he had complete confidence in his officer, that he could not lie, **and that the confusion may be a misunderstanding.** Then, with time, the matter was resolved. All three leaders were transferred from their present place of posting to other branches despite with resistance.

However, they did not join. Many agitations started, followed by a legal fight, and the matter went to the High Court. With time, issues got settled in favour of the Bank, and they all had to join at the new place of posting. The legal battle was fought for about three/four years. There were three primary petitions from our Region. One of the petitions had all India impact, which was related to the seniority of the employees. After the amalgamation of ENBI, the Central Government notified that the service of ENBI employees would be considered half for seniority purposes. One of the employees posted in the Bathinda region challenged the same notification in the High Court. Although the petition in the High Court was followed up and taken care of by the Head Office, as the petition was filed from our region, it was Bathinda Region's responsibility to follow it up. The other two petitions related to the transfer of employees, and one was about the recruitment of a guard. In the petition the guard, raised the matter of issue an appointment letter (who was selected by ENBI, but the appointment letter was not issued). In the petition relating to the appointment of a guard, the ENBI union managed to issue the notice under criminal proceedings against our Regional Manager. All leaders came to our office, met me, and showed me the court order. After seeing the order, I was slightly confused and immediately informed the Regional Manager. This was a matter of concern for us. The Regional Manager advised me to discuss the matter with a dealing advocate. However, after discussion with the concerned advocate, it was decided to fight the issue; accordingly, the bank filed the reply, and on the next hearing (I was present in the court), the honourable court dismissed the petition of the guard. The rest of the things closed automatically. I took a sigh of relief. The other petition of transfer matters was never decided during my stay in the Regional Office.

In another matter, also a High Court case, when I was discussing the matter with an advocate at Chandigarh, he advised me that a reply is required to be filed the next day itself under the signature of the Regional Manager. My worry was how would I get the signature of Regional Manager whereas the reply would be prepared in the evening. The advocate advised me to get RM's signature on the last page and handed over the papers to me. Again, I was confused, and two questions arose: first, how could I request the RM to sign on the last pages, and whether or not he would sign? Requiring a senior officer to sign on the last pages is a tricky question for a junior officer. I discussed the matter with the Regional Manager from Chandigarh on the telephone. He did not respond well, but with fear in my mind, I reached his house at 9 pm. I had not spoken any words but only handed over the papers. **He signed the documents on the last page and said he had complete confidence in me.** Those are very encouraging words. The next day, a reply was filed in court, and I showed all the signed papers to my Regional Manager.

However, in the other petition relating to seniority, although Region and Zone put in much effort, the Head Office HRD Department played the central role. In the high court, the case used to be listed daily after lunch till it was decided. A lengthy argument from all parties and senior counsels was held, and I remained in the court on all the days, witnessed the proceedings, and listened to the arguments. Finally, the matter was decided in March 1996 by the Honourable Court.

taking part in a sports activity at the bank

Take Aways

- Every problem has a solution, and we can only solve it if we have a positive attitude to our jobs.
- Win the confidence of your seniors and juniors.

CHAPTER 5

PROMOTION AS MANAGER

PROMOTION TEST

When the seniority petition was decided in March 1996, the promotion process (which was kept in abeyance for the past three years) of PNB started for different grades, which were held up due to the decision of the seniority petition. I was a scale one officer, and a circular for promotion was issued in July 1996 from JMG scale 1 to MMG scale 2 with the cut date 30.06.1989. As I was promoted to JMG Scale 1 on 17.07.1989, I was not eligible for the selection process. Suddenly, the process was stopped when a review petition was filed in the Supreme Court, and it took another three months to decide on the matter. The next instruction came in October 1996, and the date was changed to 30.09.1989. As such, I became eligible for the promotion process.

The promotion process has been delayed for the last four years due to the NBI merger and various court cases. Five batches from 1985 to 1989 of scale one officers competed. There was a very tough competition, as approximately 2000 candidates competed for less than 400 posts.

A lot of preparation and a lot of study had to be done. I qualified for the promotion and was placed at number 5 in Punjab, and a total of 6 candidates qualified from Bathinda Region, and I was number 1 in my region. As per the transfer policy, postings on promotion were to be done as per the merit of the promotion result. Therefore, I was sure I would be posted in the Bathinda Region even if there was only one vacancy because of my rank. When orders were received, all the candidates with lower merits than me were posted in Bathinda, but I was shifted to Ludhiana. I was astonished by this discrimination, and I decided to fight against it. I even appeared before my Zonal Manager. I requested him to reverse the orders as these were issued against the policy, and even unions came to my rescue. The Zonal Manager reviewed my orders, and I was transferred back to the Bathinda Region and posted in the BUDLADHA Branch as Incumbent-in-Charge.

A CHALLENGE BRANCH BUDLADHA

Before my joining, the Budladha branch was a non-performing unit. There has been negative growth in business for the last 4/5 years. The business was stagnant at Rs 11 crore. During that period, three managers were transferred, having a tenure of around one year. It was very challenging to run this office. I observed the branch working in the Regional Office, as the branch was under the administrative control of the Bathinda Region. It was a very notorious branch in terms of industrial relations and customer service. During various review meetings where I was always present, the functioning of the branch was very well known to me. I knew the ailments in the functioning of the branch, particularly customer service, staff issues, having one union but two groups fighting with each other in petty matters, rising non-performing assets, a large number of complaints pouring from customers on the non-resolved issues, etc. Last was when Oriental Bank of Commerce opened a branch in the town, providing excellent service. All customers preferred that bank as the PNB branch's business was shifting to that bank.

After my joining, I observed all these ailments practically and also observed that local customers and commission agents had no faith in the branch and were not ready to deal with the branch; even in one meeting, one high net-worth customer told me, "Manager sahib you have come to my shop, please take tea or cold drinks, but I will not come to the bank to get my clothes torn in the branch by the staff."

The other major challenge was from the Oriental Bank of Commerce, the branch that opened two years ago. The manager was very aggressive. I listed all the problems hindering the smooth running of the branch. The first issue I wanted to resolve was customer service and restoring customers' faith.

IMPROVING CUSTOMER SERVICE AND CHANGING THE ATTITUDE OF STAFF

I decided to address and resolve the customer service problem to enhance the bank's image in the area. I knew that without significant improvement in customer service, we would not be able to move an inch toward the right development track. Although my predecessor also worked on this front, he spent only six months in the branch.

I worked on three strategies: first sensitizing the staff, then meeting the customers, and frequently coming to the banking hall to ensure that customers are taken care of and their work is done to their satisfaction. I started the staff meetings fortnightly, sensitizing them about the branch's reputation in the field and telling them that the branch's reputation reflects the staff's reputation. I further said to them that without improving customer service, we wouldn't be able to enhance the business of the Bank for which we all had been posted here. Almost all clerical staff were local, and they knew every customer. After the first staff meeting ended and all staff had left for the day, one of our guards, Sh Tara Singh, came to my cabin and asked me if he could help the branch with business. I told him that he was the first person with whom customers would interact or face at the branch gate. At that time, he said, "Sir, I am so important, now I will change myself and work for the bank's growth. I joined the Bank 10 years ago, and no one told me I could do this. You are the first person who has told me about the contribution of business."

Head Cashier Sh Joginder Singh was the other resourceful, well-known personality in the area, who also enjoyed an excellent reputation among customers and was always ready to help. He always remained with me for customer service. He was an asset for the branch, and I got maximum return from this asset for the growth of the business.

The officer and supervisory staff were also very well known to me, as all were my bosses/seniors when I was in the clerical cadre in the Mansa branch. They all were with me for support, but they had their limitations, which I knew. When you know all these things about your staff, you must adjust to get work done from them. All were very helpful and cooperative, but one thing was in their mind: although the Manager had started the hard work, whether the Manager would be successful because of minimal branch experience in the officer cadre. There were also some so-called leaders in the branch; some staff members had closed minds in their approach, and they thought every customer was wrong. I had to handle all these issues tactfully to run the show.

Initially, there were many problems, but my officer staff helped me immensely, particularly Sh K S Mittal and Sh Darshan Garg. With following my actions, I started to improve customer service, i.e., fortnightly staff meetings to sensitize the staff and daily meetings with 3-4 customers after banking hours continued. After six months, some change was visible, satisfying me that my strategies were working. The efforts of staff meetings, regular meetings with customers daily, and my intervention in the banking hall during customer service hours continued till my stay in the branch, which helped me to improve the customer service and resultant increase in business of the branch.

ACCOUNT OF BLOCK DEVELOPMENT OFFICER

During that time, Saturdays used to be half-day, and branch working was up to noon. One day at around 12.30 pm, I received a telephone call, and the caller enquired if the bank could open his account. I said yes, but he again enquired if someone from the bank could visit his house to open the account, and I again said yes. (As already discussed, we did not miss any opportunity for business) Then a reply came from the other side, saying that he was the Block Development Officer, had just joined Budladha, and wanted to open the account. As the system was manual, I prepared one passbook and also had a cheque book, marked the account number, and reached his office. (My scooter was always parked in the branch for field duty purposes). The account of BDPO was opened, and the passbook pand cheque book were handed over to him immediately. He was pleased, and after taking a cup of tea when I had to leave, he gave me another draft of Rs 50 lacs of development funds, and an official account of BDPO was also opened. All these funds were to be transferred to the gram panchayats of different villages. As a result, the branch could open accounts for all gram panchayats in the area. He said he wanted to know whether PNB was active and showed his satisfaction. He had a special attachment to PNB, as before joining BDPO, he worked there.

ISSUE OF DRAFT

One day, a draft was to be issued drawn on the Sangrur branch but was issued drawn on the Bathinda branch. The party took the delivery of the draft, and the amount was equivalent to the cost of one diesel oil tanker filled by oil companies for filling stations, which was sent to Sangrur for filling. When the tanker was filed, and the draft was handed over to the oil company, they impounded it as the draft was drawn on Bathinda instead of Sangrur. The party immediately approached the bank and requested to issue a new draft against the cancellation of the draft, which was with the tanker driver at Sangrur. The same would be available on reaching the tanker in Budladha. The party also showed helplessness in depositing the amount for the issue of a fresh draft. I allowed the issue of the draft against the cancellation of the draft, which was in the tanker driver's possession, on the party's assurance that the same would be handed over to the bank. In the evening, at 6 o'clock, the party rushed to the bank with the original draft and was very thankful. Party also assured more business for the branch.

There was a cash credit account with a limit of Rs 2 lakh. The party had the dealership of MRF tires. The party has been dealing with the branch for the last 4/5 years. The proprietor's residence was near the branch. Two/three days a week, he used to come to the branch before lunchtime to deposit cash and submit a request for the issue of draft fav. MRF ltd. The clerical staff working on the seat was a local person and a neighbor of the party. One day, a situation arose when the party came to the bank at 1.55 pm and deposited the cash in the account for the issue of the draft. The staff, adhering to their routine, threw away his draft application and insisted on his coming to the bank before lunchtime. The party, feeling unheard, requested a change in the staff's approach. Recognizing the need for intervention, I stepped in, released his voucher for the draft issue, and asked him to collect the draft at 3 pm, thereby resolving the problem and reinforcing the staff's role in such incidents.

After lunch, all the staff started to work on their seats, and I called the concerned clerical staff inside my chamber. I told him that he had lifelong relations with the party as his neighbor, whereas my relations were only professional. This person would join on all occasions at his house. But his behavior today towards him was improper. He thought for a while and expressed regret. However, I advised him to contact his neighbor and express regret about his behavior. When the party came to the office at 3 pm to collect the draft, I observed both sitting together and having tea.

RATE OF INTEREST

Another exciting story is a cash credit limit of Rs 70 lac in the branch for the cotton ginning and pressing factory. The party was enjoying an excellent reputation in the bank and the market. The area was very fertile for cotton crops. Our branch was charging one percent more interest in the account than the ROI offered by other banks in the town. At that time, ledgers were manual. I assured the party that the bank would not dishonor his cheques. The ledger keeper and officer were advised that cheques should be cleared in this account, and only when they exceed the limit the party should be informed before dishonoring the cheque.

Mostly at 3 o'clock, the account was reported overdrawn. A telephone call/message was delivered daily, and the party would immediately deposit cash and drafts to approximately Rs. 20 lacs in the account. Every day in the evening, the balance remained around Rs 50 lakh in the account. The party's reputation in the market was very high as cheques were never dishonored, and the party was cheaply getting the raw material, i.e., cotton.

One day, the party approached me with a sanction letter of Rs 70 lakh from the State Bank of Patiala, and the rate of interest offered was 1% less than PNB. The party requested that 1% less interest make a big difference and asked to reduce the interest, or they had no alternative but to shift the account. I patiently listened to what he was saying, and he was also correct in asking for reduced ROI. I offered him a cup of tea; over a cup of tea, I told him that he knew that no cheque of his firm was ever dishonored, and the firm is enjoying an excellent reputation in the market because the bank never dishonored any cheque and as a result, he was getting stocks at cheaper rates. Because of this, he was earning more, so the bank charged the excess interest. After finishing his tea, he listened patiently and told me that as I had clarified the matter, he would not shift to another bank and tore the sanction letter from the State Bank of Patiala in my presence. He smiled and left the office.

OLD SAVING ACCOUNT

One day, a person with an old passbook in his hand, having only a balance of Rs 5, approached the guard at the gate. He was in a pressing situation, having just sold his house and needing to deposit the sale proceeds. Recognizing the urgency, the guard immediately guided the customer to me. I promptly checked his passbook, and the account was running. Without delay, the branch deputed a cashier and guard to collect the cash, which was Rs 6 lac then, and the entire amount was placed in FD. This swift response resolved the customer's immediate need and demonstrated our bank's proactive and customer-centric approach.

A father and son from a nearby village visited our branch one day. The son was NRI. The father had one fixed deposit receipt of Rs. 25000 with him, and they wanted to get it encashed. I offered them a cup of tea and requested to continue the deposit, but they insisted on payment. They said that they needed money. Understanding their situation, I told them that as his son was NRI, he had no shortage of money and that he should continue the deposit. Despite my many requests, they did not agree. So, I got up from my seat, and FD was passed for payment, and Rs 25000 plus interest was handed over to them. After receiving the money, they again sat down and requested to issue the FD. I was surprised, but they also asked to open one savings fund account for his son. I filled up the necessary documents, and when I asked about the deposit, it was Rs 6 lac, which was lying in their bag. They told me that they were going to the State Bank of Patiala for a deposit along with the FD of 25000, but as they found our services very satisfactory, they decided to deposit the entire amount in PNB.

GUN LICENSE

I joined the branch on 12.05.1997, and an inspection of the branch was going on. During the inspection, it was observed that one gun license had expired in 1975. This matter was a very strange one and serious also. So, I started the process for renewal after consulting with the security officer and license issuing authorities, DM Mansa. But the file was not moving. As I sometimes travelled from Bathinda to Budladha, one day on the train, I met the superintendent of the DM office; after two or three meetings, we became very well-known to each other. So, I approached him for renewal of my gun license, and after going through the file, he told me that it was a serious issue. the present DM was stringent, and he might send me to jail, so please wait.

He told me not to follow up and that he would get things cleared at the appropriate time. The DM was transferred after three/four months, and a new DM joined. The superintendent put up the file and got the notice issued for appearing before the DM. On the given date, I appeared, and DM, who was very lovely in behaviour, told me that bank people were generally very disciplined, so why this had happened. I clarified that it is an old issue. I have just joined the branch and am taking steps for correction. DM ordered renewal but also advised that a note of caution be issued to BM. After 30 days, the gun license was renewed, and I was issued a note of caution by DM, although I had taken the issues to the appropriate authority and follow up.

LEADERSHIP

The other task in the branch was to improve the working of so-called leaders. I tried to make them understand things somewhat, and there was some improvement. Wherever it was felt necessary, I handled them with an iron hand to get the desired results. Anyhow, they showed improvement to the extent it was needed. The total deposit of the branch was approximately Rs. 810 lakhs, and we had an account of one religious institution having a good deposit with the branch. Due to their requirement, they withdrew a significant amount, which was a big setback to the branch, and all the staff were upset. I also had the same feeling but was happy now that the staff had started understanding the importance of business. There was a significant change in the staff's thought process. This was the need of the hour, not the business. The positive change in staff morale after my leadership efforts underscores the crucial role of effective leadership in a branch banking.

I wrote a DO letter to my Regional Manager about the deposit withdrawal in one account and efforts being put in by me to improve the working of the branch, and I got the following reply from the Regional Manager, which I quote:

"I have full faith in the leadership of the present branch manager."

This was a great moral booster for the branch. In September 1997 our Regional Manager visited our branch and held a customer meeting after a long time. About 30-40 customers were invited. Before the meeting, I was sceptical that in the open house, one could ask anything and question the authorities. However, customers were satisfied with the smooth sailing, and our Regional Manager was happy. During the meeting, customers praised the efforts put in by the branch to improve customer service and development efforts. So, from the customer service point of view, the branch was on the right track, but it was still an ongoing process, and a daily watch was required.

HANDLING NPA

The next big challenge was to handle the NPA, which was 33% of the total credit of the branch; besides, around 33% of accounts were in the irregular category. There were 26 decreed accounts in the branch that were over 20 years old. A list of all NPA and irregular accounts was prepared village-wise so that when any officer visits the town, he might have first-hand information about all irregular and NPA borrowers. The team was consisting of Sh K S Mittal, Sh Harmesh Garg, and above all, Sh G S Deol, the Agriculture Officer. I also, on a fortnightly basis, started to review every account. In the first meeting, I had advised the staff to prepare a new ledger for the decreed accounts by calculating the dues as per court orders, but the staff had the opinion that we could not do anything as all cases were in court. I firmly believed that everything could be sorted out, out of court by dialogue, and advised them to look into my suggestions. I, along with my team, started to meet borrowers and issue notices. The impact had started to come out because of the notices and contacts made by us.

When the first notice was sent in all decreed accounts as per revised calculations, one farmer turned up and showed his desire to clear the account, but his apprehension was about the court case filed by the bank against him. I assured him that the case would be withdrawn and that I would sign all papers as the branch manager. He agreed and deposited the money, and the account was adjusted. This was the first success of recovery of 20-year-old NPA account. The branch received many letters of appreciation from authorities, and the staff was also charged. We continued our efforts for other accounts. On an average, in every crop season, we adjusted one account out of the remaining 25 accounts. During my three and half years of tenure, about 14 accounts were adjusted. There are numerous stories I will share, two or three of which are here.

I contacted all these borrowers regularly. The house of one of the borrowers was on the road in a village, and he used to sit outside his home on a cot after four in the evening. Mostly, I went to villages in the evening to meet borrowers, and I never stopped at his house but always said Sat Sri Akal while moving on the two-wheeler. It continued for almost two years. One day, he came to the bank, and I extended all respect to him as he was of my father's age. He was pleased and requested that his account be closed. I calculated the amount as per court order, and the account was adjusted. Then he told me that he had never come to his house for recovery but always respected him by saying Sat Sri Akal in front of his house, and one day, his daughter-in-law asked him why the bank manager always said Sat Sri Akal to him. Are there any bank dues? Then, he decided to close the account. He was pleased with how follow-up was made in his account for recovery.

In one of the accounts, the borrower's land was on the way to his Village. I along with AO; whenever contacted him, he always met us in the field, and we had never gone to his house. We have been following up on recovery for the last two years, but there has been no progress. One day, we both went to meet them, but he was not in the field, so we decided to go to his house in the village. When we reached his house, a young lady enquired about our visit. We told her the details of the account. She was stunned and offered us a cup of tea, which we declined with all due respect to her because she was alone at home, but she addressed us as brothers and told us that we need not come again for this purpose. After we came back, the account was adjusted within next ten days. So, there were many such interesting stories about these old accounts and how they were adjusted.

ACHIEVING TARGETS AND GETTING NEW BUSINESS

One thing: I always maintained excellent relations with all the sarpanches of the villages of my branch area and BDPO. I give all my regards and thanks to Head Cashier Sh Joginder Singh, who is not presently among us, with whose help I was introduced to many good customers in villages.

On 31st March 1999, it was the annual closing day. The branch had to achieve many targets, including yearly closing, but the branch was missing the main deposit target despite our best efforts. All staff members were upset because, despite team efforts, the branch could not achieve the budget. Still, being the leader gave them consolation, and after totally surrendering to fate, I advised the staff to close the books at 12.30 pm (Saturday). Then, suddenly, one staff member (the union leader) came to my chamber in a delighted mood and said we had achieved the target. A draft of Rs 40 lac was in his hands for deposit in the current account of a party. The total atmosphere of the branch changed to a party atmosphere, and the branch achieved all the targets. JADON RAB DINDA CHHAT PARR KE.

All staff members were fully charged and sensitized by holding meetings, seeking business cooperation, and improving customer service.

Those days, the focus was on non-interest income as usual, and one of the heads of non-interest income was earning draft commission. I approached many parties to get the draft issue business for the branch. There were five fuel filling stations, and no one got the drafts issued by PNB because of the poor customer service and higher draft commission rate. Providing better customer service in the branch was in my hands, but not the commission rate. Our new Regional Manager had just joined. One day, one party came to the branch and requested that he is ready to switch to PNB for the issue of drafts, but the commission should be matched with other banks. I offered him a cup of tea, and had a telephone talk with my RM, and requested him to allow concession on the draft commission rate to the party, and the branch would send the proposal. The reply from the Regional Manager was, "Mr. Mann, you have been allowed to extend the concession starting today. Just send a letter to confirm my telephone conversation". That was a turning point for me, and the message went to the market. Within one month, three parties out of five were dealing with PNB. The branch had given the best service to these parties. There are many other success stories of the branch.

Once, I appeared in court as a witness from the bank side in a suit filed account. During cross-examination, the advocate asked me several questions irrelevant to the case, but when I objected, he again requested two or three questions. The court cautioned him, but he continued and concluded. Then he privately told me sorry and said his client was standing there.

FILING OF THE SUIT IN THE STANDARD ACCOUNT

While working in the branch in the usual course of business, a tractor loan was sanctioned. The party had a landholding of about 25 acres, and the tractor was high-end. They were regularly deposing their installments. But on two occasions, they failed. First, they could not produce joint registration of the tractor with the bank, and second, they would not sign the balance confirmation letter. Despite our efforts to make them understand to sign the BC letter, the party did not sign. What surprised me that he was an advocate by profession. I could not understand why he was a reluctant to sign the BC letter. The account was a standard category. Whatever installments were deposited by the party, all the vouchers were signed by someone else. Although the account was a standard category, the bank had to file the suit to save limitations.

DEFAMATION CASE AGAINST OUR COLLEAGUE

Before I joined the branch, one assistant manager, Sh G K Mittal, worked there. There was one party that had some grievances against his services. The party filed a defamation case against Shri. Mittal. The court admitted the case as a personal case against the officer. The bank was giving no legal/monetary help. He had to defend the case at his own cost. The issue came to my notice. Some staff members told me that the party was habitual in doing this. So, I decided, being the incumbent, to help our colleague to come out of this case.

I tried to contact the party through local staff many times, but he was not ready to meet. Several efforts were made in six months. After six months, I got a break. I met the party at his shop. He kept complaining about Sh Mittal, and I was just on the receiving end. I remained quiet because I did not want to break the talks for an essential purpose. After that, two or three more meetings were held, and I pleaded with the party that we should not go to that extent. I tried to tell him that service issues are always present in the banking industry and can be resolved by sitting together. We should not go on a personal basis. After three months of effort, he agreed to meet Shri Mittal to resolve the issue. Shri Mittal was called from other station to fix the problem, but again, he somehow didn't meet for one reason or another. The exercise became futile. But I had decided not to leave the matter here. Again, efforts were made to contact the party, and I met him. I advised him it was not fair from his side not to meet Shri Mittal after calling him from 70 km away. After that, a meeting was fixed on another date, but I clarified to him that the matter had to be resolved on that date. Mr. Mittal came on the fixed date. We all sat together for one hour and had a cup of tea. The joint memorandum of understanding was signed to withdraw the court case. Our colleague and I had a sign of relief.

Kissan millan programme branch office Budladha

I worked in the branch for about three and half years, and business increased from Rs. 11 Cr to Rs. 19 Cr. The NPA of the branch reduced from 33% to 6%. Also, there were no complaints of the branch from any side. The branch had an excellent reputation in the area, particularly from a customer service point of view. The branch was also refurnished during my stay, giving it a new look. The other highly appreciated officers who contributed are Sh Harmesh Kumar Garg, Sh Vinod Kumar, Sh BR Singla, and all the award staff and support staff. I was transferred and posted as Manager at branch Civil Lines Bathinda on 19.01.2001

BATHINDA CIVIL LINES

I worked in the branch Bathinda civil lines for one year only and was promoted to Sr Manager and posted at Lucknow on 20.01. 2002. When I joined BO Bathinda Civil Lines, the branch's business was Rs. 11 Cr. The branch's deposit was stagnant for the last three years at Rs. 8.25 Cr, and the target was Rs. 10 Cr. for March 2001. After going through the entire business profile and budgets of the branch on 31st January 2001, I called the second man of the branch to discuss the strategy to achieve the branch target, but (with all respect to him, a very close friend of mine even today) he stated that for the last three years, the deposit has not increased from Rs. 8.25 Cr even to Rs. 8.50 Cr, how it can be increased to 10 crores in two months. But again, I adopted the same strategy (as of the early branch) of customer service and staff meetings. To our surprise, we touched the figure of 10.30 Cr on 31st March. Every week, the deposit was increased by Rs. 20 lacs. Even the second man of the branch expressed his surprise about how the deposits were growing. All the other staff, too, were surprised how the deposit was increasing, but I knew the secret behind it.

In this branch, the other problem was the large number of irregular accounts. The major problem was three big accounts, all about 35 to 40 km from Bathinda and going in different directions. Considering the various directions and distance, a car was required to contact these borrowers. So, I requested the RM to allow a taxi to contact these borrowers; the Regional Manager (RM) was kind enough to allow the car to visit these borrowers. (As per guidelines, permission is to be sought for every trip, but this permission was up to 31st March 2001 for any number of trips to visit these borrowers.) Resultantly, out of three accounts, two were saved from NPA. The recovery target of the branch's NPA accounts for 31st March 2001 was Rs. 15 lacs, but I managed to recover only Rs 1.5 lac.

CALCULATED RISK

While working in the branch, sometimes we have to take calculated risks in the bank's interest, for customer service, to hold the customer with the bank, and to increase the business. After joining the branch a few days ago, one of our colleagues introduced to the branch a well-known doctor of the city who was renovating a hospital on G T Road, and he was in requirement of a loan. When asked about the loan amount, he smiled and said to the extent of branch power. He handed over to me the required documents and title deeds of the hospital; the value of the properties was very much above the loan amount. Without going into much of the formalities, the branch credited the loan amount to his account, and he was pleased. As a result, he shifted all his family accounts to our branch—a good chunk of the deposit.

One day at 3 pm, I received a telephone call from the doctor. He enquired about the sanction of a house loan. He requested a loan of Rs 5 lac, which was in the branch's power and requested sanction and disbursement on that day. But he again asked that he require a loan immediately as he was standing in court for registration and requested to send a pay order immediately. The formalities would be completed the next day. The branch immediately prepared the pay order and sent it to the doctor in court through a peon. I requested the doctor to purchase three stamp papers for the agreement for that day. At 5 pm, the doctor's assistant came to the branch to get the required documents checklist. After three days, the doctor and his wife visited the branch to sign all the documents and the other required papers. He was pleased with the way the bank had solved his problem. Now, after that, all his banking business was with our branch. The decision to disburse the house loan without documents and security was taken based on the reputation of the doctor and the value of security already with the bank. The doctor maintains excellent relations with PNB staff even today after 23 years.

When I was promoted as Sr. Manager, and it was my last working day in the branch, at 1 pm, one lady customer, having a current account with the branch for the previous ten years, came to my chamber and requested 60 leaves of cheques. When I inquired about it, she said she had availed a car loan of 6 lac from TATA finance. Then, I asked her to sit down and ordered a cup of tea. Then, we calculated the economics of the loan from TATA and PNB. PNB loan was cheap. But she said that PNB would take many days to sanction the loan, and she required it the same day. I promised to sanction it the same day, and she agreed to avail of a loan from PNB. I always maintained some stamp papers in the branch for emergency use. The loan officer got signed the documents and handed over the draft to her in 15 minutes. She was pleased. Whatever the pending issues were in the file, I noted them and requested my successor to complete it.

There were 5/6 cash credit limits of govt contractors in the branch, and these limits were occasionally overdrawn as per requirements and within bank rules. One day, in a limit of Rs 25 lacs, having a balance of Rs 30 lac, i.e., 20% overdrawn, the party came to the branch and requested a bank guarantee of Rs 7 lacs. The party had no BG limit, and all BGs were issued to all parties when required against the cash margin. He requested that a bank guarantee be issued without security. He pleaded that upon submitting the guarantee, he would get a cheque of Rs 29 lac from the govt department, which was ready. We all believed that by evening party would get the cheque of Rs 29 lac, so we overdrawn the limit by another Rs 7 lac and created security for the BG. Accordingly, BG was issued.

In the evening, he did not turn up; even after three days, he did not turn up and was not responding to the calls. The matter was of great concern for the bank. After three days, we received a call, and he informed us that the engineer who had to sign the cheque had left for Delhi because of the death of his mother. On his joining, he would sign the cheque. After 7/8 days, he turned up with a cheque of Rs 29 lac, and all limits were adjusted on realization. As it was being overdrawn beyond power, I informed my Regional Manager of the entire matter and requested for confirmation of the action. He agreed, and action was confirmed.

In another case, one of the borrowers, a govt contractor, received a govt. cheque of Rs 37 lac which was drawn from another bank branch in Chandigarh. As it was a govt cheque, it was within the branch's power to discount it, and it was discounted and immediately dispatched to the Chandigarh branch for presentation to the drawee bank. The whole process till realization was taking 12-15 days. But we had a different arrangement; the Sr. Manager working at the Chandigarh branch was well known to me, so this cheque took 6-7 days to realize. When any cheque is cleared, he immediately faxes the realization advice, and the entry is reversed. Thus, saving one week's interest. After 6/7 days of sending the cheque, the branch telephoned the Chandigarh branch about the realization of the cheque, and a reply came that the cheque had been returned. Without knowing the reasons, there was panic as the amount was huge. I immediately called the borrower and informed him, but he said it was impossible to return the cheque because of funds, but there may be other reasons. The borrower also said that he had another cheque of Rs 45 lac and was coming to the branch. Then I called the Chandigarh branch and enquired about the reason for the return, and the reply came that the name of the bank's drawee branch was not mentioned, and as such, it was returned. Then I requested the Sr. Manager not to return the cheque but to wait for one hour. Meanwhile, the party deposited the other cheque drawn by the same drawer, and the same drawee and the name of the branch was mentioned as Sector 22. I requested the Chandigarh branch to represent the cheque to the Sector 22 branch of the drawee Bank. After three days, the cheque was cleared. Then, the branch purchased other cheques and mobilized more business and income. However, the situation could have become difficult had the cheque been returned and reported to the controlling authority. The branch just handled the issue in time.

NPA BUDGET

In May 2001, I got an appreciation letter from RM stating that I had achieved the NPA recovery budget target for March 2001. at the same time, the branch could manage only Rs 1.50 lac recovery against the targets of 15 lac. I called the dealing manager in the Regional Office and explained the position; he replied that it was better to talk to the Regional Manager. One day, on my visit to the Regional Office, I discussed the matter with the RM, and he advised me, **"Achievements letters are given on the efforts put in by a person, not based on how much figures he has achieved."** I was delighted, and my morale was very high. My last closing in the branch was 30.09.2001, and the branch had achieved a total business of Rs. 19 Cr, which had increased from Rs. 11 Cr from the date of joining, i.e.20.01.2001.

Take Aways

— **Before starting work at the new branch, understand the working of the branch/business/and problems**

— **The focus should be on having satisfied customers, and the attitude of the staff should be positive towards customers.**

— **Always be proactive for business.**

— **Regularly be in touch with customers and NPA customers**

— **Help your colleagues if you are in such a position.**

— **Always take calculated risks for business, and decisions should be made to protect the bank's interests.**

CHAPTER 6

PROMOTION AS SENIOR MANAGER

POSTING AND JOINING

I was promoted to Senior Manager on 02.01.2002 and was allocated to Inspection & Control Division at Head Office. So, I was relieved on 17.01.2002.

New Experience to work as an Auditor – **POSTING AND JOINING**

About 80% of candidates promoted to Senior Manager from Punjab Zone were allotted to the Inspection and Control Division at HO for audit work and were to report to the Regional Staff College Panchkula. Along with other candidates, I joined Panchkula for one week of training. During the training, everyone was worried about posting rather than training. Everyone was trying his best to get the nearest posting. (As all candidates were under Head Office, the posting could happen anywhere in the country)

While sitting in my room, I also thought of posting, but I had no approach to work; then, I felt no problem. Where was my food? I had to go there. (Jetha Dane Outie hi khene…) I mentally prepared myself to happily accepting the posting where it was. Then, I was very much relieved from all worries.

On the last day of training, Sh S.K. Roy AGM, from Head Office, addressed the candidates and made it clear that, keeping in view the vacancies, all will be posted in East UP Zone. I had seen some candidates weeping loudly and pleading for a soft posting on the grounds of family, health, etc., which was expected of all. For a moment, I thought about the army men defending our borders at the Kargil Hills, far away from their families and having no possibility of even a telephonic connection with their families. In contrast, we would have an excellent house, telephone links with family, and no problem availing of leave as and when required. This thought gave me more strength to overcome my hesitation to move out because of the transfer. I was, therefore, mentally prepared to move anywhere in the country. AGM was calling each one personally. When my turn came to plead my case for posting with my other friends, we requested that the bank may post us anywhere. There was no issue; we three may posted on the same station so that we could stay together.

AGM was pleased to listen to this; when we got the posting after one week, we three were posted in Lucknow, a lovely and historical city with good branches and PNB having an excellent reputation in Lucknow.

Now, a question arose: where is Lucknow, and how can I reach it? One of my senior colleagues asked me if I knew how to see the railway timetable. I said, no, sir, then he advised me to go to the railway station and have a copy of the same. Then, he taught me how to find trains at a particular station. This map taught me where Lucknow is and how to get it. We five people went together to Lucknow by the same train from Delhi, i.e., the Gomti Express.

We had received feedback from other colleagues that we should be alert at a railway station in UP as the chances of looting were higher. We also got some references for a night stay in a hotel near the railway station. The train reached Lucknow railway station at 11 pm, and we de-boarded the train and came out of the railway station with our bag and baggage. We had all moved out of Bathinda, crossed the Delhi for the first time, and knew nothing about the rest of India. As we came out, we were surrounded by several people, and I thought, as was the feedback given to us, they would now loot us. They were pulling our luggage and us, a bizarre situation. We rebuked them and showed our strength at the end, and they all ran away. We sighed in relief and called the rickshaw puller, loaded our luggage, and reached the hotel we had the reference for. It had come to our notice later that they (to whom we understood as looters) were trying to get the passengers, as when these passengers would go to a hotel, the hotel would offer some commission to Ricksha Wala. They were not looters. Our hotel was terrible and dirty, and we were not ready to step in, but keeping in view the circumstances, we stayed there. The following day, we came out to have a cup of tea and asked some passersby about a hotel for tea, and he replied that on the left side was a Hindu hotel, and on the right side was a Muslim hotel. These words were heard for the first time, and we were astonished. But he again replied, "Sir, here is the system. It may not be in Punjab" that politics divides the people, their shops, and eating places.

Then, we inquired about the addresses of our branches and were advised to ride a sumo jeep to reach there. We were astonished to learn that the sumo fare would be Rs 300-400. When we reached the nearest sumo jeep and asked about the fare, he told us Rs 5 per passenger, and we all went to our respective branches and joined.

STAY ARRANGEMENTS

We three got a house on lease near my branch, Vidhan Saba Marg Lucknow, on Cantonment Road. It was a good house on the first floor with three bedrooms and a big lobby. All bedding was with us, and we opened bedding there; one of my colleagues put his bed near a corner and stated 'Konje and Bunje' (set in a corner and on the floor) as he was earlier branch manager and now was an auditor. One maid was arranged for cleaning and washing utensils. We also allocated our duties for household jobs as all three had not shifted the families. My duty was to arrange milk and boil it, after dinner then served milk to all three in the evening. I prepared morning tea; one had to arrange vegetables and cook them. The third candidate is to cook the rotis/parathas in the evening and morning. We arranged some furniture from our staff members, and some was purchased second-hand, including a fridge. Even in summer vacations, all three families visited Lucknow for one month, and the children enjoyed it. Along with families, we visited Ayodhya and other places in Lucknow. With families, we were 12 people. Breakfast, lunch, and dinner all were served like a Langer with self-service, and all enjoyed very well. There was an Atta Chakki nearby, and we used to frequently visit at that shop to buy items. The owner was also having PCO, where we regularly went to make phone calls. He was very friendly and became our friend. There was another shop for sweets where we arranged milk daily and sometimes twice a week morning snacks like Aloo Puri and Jalebies. Sometimes, he would also manage the keys to our house. Many persons were posted from Punjab in the east zone. Their controlling office was in Lucknow, so they all approached us for any issue with the controlling office, and if anyone had to stay in Lucknow, our house was always available, so in a week consistently, there was one guest with us, particularly on Saturday or Sunday.

One money box was kept in the house, and everyone had to put Rs 1500 in it at the beginning of every month. That box financed the entire household's expenditures.

I remained posted in Lucknow until June 2003 and worked in two branches as an auditor. One was Lucknow Vidhan Saba Marg, and another was Deoria near Gorakhpur, about 300 km from Lucknow. There were many sweet and sour memories of my stay there. Also, I got the opportunity to visit many cities and towns of UP, particularly Ayodhya, Gorakhpur, Gonda, Balarampur, Jhansi, Kanpur, and many others. During the posting, we visited our hometown once a month. Senior managers in both branches were very kind, and they extended all cooperation. I also extended all help to the branches for business growth.

TRANSFER TO JALANDHAR

While posted in Lucknow, we felt some difficulties due to children's education and other social responsibilities at home. After a stay of more than one year, we decided to meet our General Manager at HO for a transfer back to our home state. As per policy, transfers are mostly affected after two years of stay or when a new batch joins. But we had completed only one year and three months, and a new batch was about to join.

We reached HO Delhi to meet the General Manager (inspection). Through his PA, all three (Sh Subash Jindal, Sh Bhushan Goyal, and me) sent a joint slip to meet the GM. We waited for one hour but were not called. We then feared that the GM would not meet us and that we would face some action as we were visiting HO without his permission. However, soon, a message came, and we three were sitting before our GM. His lovely behavior towards us amazed us, and he listened to all our problems. We also requested that, at present, we are arranging to visit our families once a month, but we desire to see the family once a week, and the bank might post us anywhere and in any capacity.GM also enquired about any of our family problems. Then my colleague Sh Jindal replied that at this age, there are expected to be several problems for all of us, but that should not be the basis for the transfer and should not hinder us from performing our duties. In this reply, our GM was pleased and assured us he would look into the issue we raised by us.

In May 2003, we received transfer orders to return to Punjab. The fact that the entire batch was also transferred back after a year indicated a shift in the bank's operational strategy, and we were ready and inspired to embrace this change.

Following the orders, I assumed the role of a Touring Sr. Inspector at the Zonal Audit Office, Jalandhar. This position, though demanding, was incredibly fulfilling. It entailed conducting annual audits in various branches of Punjab, a responsibility I undertook with unwavering dedication and meticulousness. This tenure, which extended until June 2007, saw me auditing numerous branches, including six branches of the Bihar zone, on two separate occasions. I also undertook 16 special investigations, each presenting a unique challenge that I approached with a steadfast commitment to uncovering the truth. In addition to fieldwork, I contributed to the Zonal Audit Office, processing Inspection Reports of diverse branches and addressing objections. This dual role not only enhanced my professional growth but also fostered a strong sense of camaraderie and unity with the staff in that office, underscoring the pivotal role of teamwork in our work.

INSPECTION OF BIHAR ZONE BRANCHES

One day, I received a telephone call from HO that I should go to Bihar to conduct an audit of 3 branches, and I was given a list of branches to choose three out of the same for this purpose. After my inquiry from sources about the location of the branches, I selected the three branches and requested for those branches. Accordingly, I got the letter for auditing these branches. After the Diwali vacation, as per the travel schedule, I reached Gaya and checked into the hotel. The first branch was near Jahanabad, about 50km from Gaya.

I presumed it would take one and a half hours to get there. At that time, there was no bus stand in the city, and buses going to Jahanabad originated from the railway station. As such, I reached the station at 9 am. The conductor told me the bus would leave by 10.30 so I waited. Booking had started in advance with seat numbers. When I purchased my ticket, he did not allot me any seat number, as the bus was going to Patna, so only Patna passengers would get seats. I was helpless. The bus took 3 hours to reach Jahanabad, and I traveled standing in the bus for about 3 hours. After that, I hired an auto and reached the branch by 2.30 pm. Only one staff member was sitting. I told him that I had come from the inspection department for an audit. He asked me to show him the authority letter and identity card. I inquired about other staff. he said he was a head cashier. The Manager was on leave, and he was running the branch. He also added that the manager was from Himachal Pradesh and would join after the holidays. To my surprise, he told me there were four holidays from the next day onward because of Chhath Puja, which was not in my knowledge. Two issues surprised me: only one staff member was running the branch, and the other was of four holidays.

So, I was stuck in the hotel room because, during the holidays, no other alternative was available. All the bazaars and all other offices were closed, and there was only a festive mood. In those days, the power position was very bad in Bihar. The power remained off all day. So, there was no fan in the hotel room, and no TV and mobile were not available on those days. The market was also closed. Now imagine how I had passed the time, but I used the opportunity to visit Bodh Gaya. I took an auto to reach Bodh Gaya. The place was beautiful, and I visited all the religious places there. It was evening when I came out and saw a massive crowd on the bank of river Surya. Even though the movement was difficult due to crowd, locals informed me that because of Chhath puja, they performed Puja on the bank of the river. I was stuck in the great rush of people going to the river for Sun Puja in the evening. Anyhow, I managed to come back.

One day, I planned to go to Patna, about 90 km from there. Locals told me that train starts at 7 am from Gaya but takes 5 hours to reach Patna, so it is better to go by bus. I boarded a bus for Patna. It started at 7.30 am, and after covering about 70km, a river was crossing the road, and the bridge had collapsed. Hence, all passengers had to cross the river on foot and board another bus on the other side, a minibus fully packed from inside to roof. I prayed to God for a safe journey and reached Patna and then to Gurudwara. I spent two hours there and also had Langer.

Now, I decided to go back by train, and I boarded the train from Patna at 5 pm, which reached Gaya at 10 pm. Again, there were no lights and fans on the train, and at every station from where the train was crossing, there was total darkness, and I was sitting alone in the bogie in total darkness. The journey was also frightful, considering Bihar's then law and order position. Thank God I reached my hotel room by 11 pm. So anyhow I spent four holidays. Meanwhile, the Manager on leave also joined, and the audit of the branch concluded in 10 days, and the report was submitted.

The next branch for audit was Tandawa near Aurangabad (in Bihar), and the Manager had come to Gaya to attend the Manager's meeting. Accordingly, we planned the journey. we started in the evening and were supposed to reach by 9 pm, but on the way, we were struck on a road due to a Road Roko agitation by villagers due to some accident, which forced us to come back to Gaya at 11 pm. The next day, we started our journey by train early in the morning and reached Aurangabad. After a brief stay and breakfast, we proceeded to branch on a motorcycle and covered 50km in 2 hours. As daily commuting was difficult, I stayed in a village where branch was situated.

There were only two/three Pacca houses in the village, and I slept on a wood bench for 3/4 nights with a mosquito net. There was no bathroom, so I bathed in the open with water from a hand pump. There was no light in the village, and one generator boy in the bank took care of my food, i.e., Dal Chawal. There was only one PCO in the town, and there was always a long queue. The villagers were nice people who gave me all the respect. They also cautioned that this village is affected by Naxalite, so I should be careful. Despite many difficulties, I enjoyed the trip and felt very happy, having lifelong memories. When I used to go to PCO for a call to my house, the villagers prioritized me. As I stayed in the village and worked from 8 am to 8 pm, I concluded the audit in 7 days.

The other branch was near Bihar Sharif, and I stayed in a hotel in the city. This area was also Naxalite affected. On the first day in the morning, I went for a morning walk, and when I came back, I found that the hotel's owner was distraught and told me not to go outside as it was dangerous. He suggested that if I had to go for a morning walk, I might walk on the back side of the hotel. As such, I followed the advice of the owner. Within ten days, the work was completed. On the last day after submitting the report, I proceeded to Patna Sahib and stayed in a hotel. The next day, early in the morning, I went to Gurudwara Sahib and spent 3 hours there; that day, Sh Guru Gobind Singh Ji's birthday was celebrated. I was daily listening to the katha by Sant Singh Maskeen; with the grace of God, I saw the Sant Ji for the first time in Gurudwara, and the day was 16th January 2005. The flight was at 3 pm, and I reached Delhi by 5 pm. Then, boarding Punjab mail, I reached Bathinda for the next assignment.

On another occasion next year, I had to visit Bihar to inspect branches again. The flight was at 11 am from Delhi via Ranchi; when it reached Ranchi, it was declared that the flight would not go to Patna because of bad weather. I had to choose either to go back to Delhi on the same flight or to Patna on a bus arranged by the airline. It was an overnight journey through the area that was severely affected by Naxalites. I was in double mind about whether to go or not to go. Then, one person approached me and asked whether I was working in PNB. I immediately asked him how he guessed I was in PNB, and then he pointed towards my bag where the bank's name was written. He was also from PNB and was the chief manager of one of the Patna branches. He was ready to go, so I also decided to go because of his advice and company.

The bus started at 9 pm. We reached Patna at 5 am, and then the train from Patna started at 6 am for Jummai Town. Despite the challenging circumstances, we persevered. He helped me get a seat in the AC chair car and told me to be careful of my bag, which may get robbed. On the way, a staff member also boarded the train from another station, and on the telephone, he asked me about my identity. I told him only one Sardar would be in the compartment, and he was pleased. He boarded the train and directly came to me. I stayed in a simple guest house for the next ten days; the caretaker was very gentle. Daily morning, he arranged for breakfast and dinner in the evening. After completing the audit, the branch manager helped me reach the next branch near Bhagalpur. Again, the branch was in a very remote area with a problematic approach, with no drinking water arrangement or food, which I managed (water and food) from my hotel while visiting the branch. After that, I audited one more branch, which was smooth. After completing the job, I returned to Punjab via Patna and Delhi.

VARIOUS INVESTIGATIONS

For three years, I regularly inspected various branches in Punjab and completed many inquiries/investigations.

In one of the branches, there were about 65 crop loan cases of Rs 50000 each with identical records of land holding on record, which generally doesn't happen. The investigation was entrusted to me, highlighting the importance of our role in maintaining the bank's integrity. When I reached the branch by the time about 13 cases were adjusted. After checking all the files and learning the facts, I visited each borrower to know the hidden facts, if any. I, along with the branch manager, visited all the borrowers, and the manager talked to the borrowers confidently and was harsh about recovery. I observed that the manager was not involved but had also been cheated. But grave irregularities existed, such as fake land records, borrowers not eligible for loans, some outside person involved in arranging the documents, etc. In my meeting with the Senior Regional Manager, I recommended that the Manager may not be transferred from the branch for at least one year, which he accepted. Generally, managers are transferred immediately upon the occurrence of this type of event. After about one year, I met the Manager when I appeared in his departmental inquiry as a Management Witness. Then he informed me that all cases had been adjusted except 6/7 cases where borrowers had expired. So, the bank's money involved has been recovered. One outsider who was working privately with a local Patwari committed this fraud. The borrowers' savings account opening forms disclosed his name to the bank. In almost 80% of cases, he had introduced the borrower, underscoring the significance of our investigations and their impact on the bank's operations.

In one of the other investigations of 94 cases of house loans, bizarre facts came to light when I went through the files. Everything in the files was perfect from a documentation point of view. Each document was properly filed, i.e., application and supporting documents, income tax return, residential proof, approved map plan, ownership proof, and perfect legal opinion. Also, there was proof of stage-wise disbursement along with an architect's certificate duly verified, and all these papers gave no doubt about any severe irregularities. My fellow inspector, Sh S C Jindal, and I visited the various sites and found the plots lying vacant, but the file showed that the houses were complete.

In the same branch, when we verified the site in another case, it was different when we compared it with the directions (north, south, east, and west) as per the registered deed. When the borrower was asked about this, who was an advocate by profession, gave a very dismal reply and said, ''APP KA SER CHKRA GYE HI GHAR SE DHOOR HOO EVERYTHING IS OKAY.' (Your head was confused as you were away from home; everything was okay.)

We stopped the verification work that day; everyone went home, but my colleague and I went to the market and purchased a compass. The next day, early morning, we visited the site and checked all the sides with a compass. Our observations were correct, and we immediately called the advocate and showed him the results. He was very depressed now. After that, I met the same advocate after many years in the CBI court, where he was accused, and I was a witness.

In many cases, all the maps and income tax returns were forged. The investigation report was submitted to HO, which was appreciated from an investigation point of view. Even later, the case was handed over to the CBI, and they also appreciated the investigation work done by the bank.

In another investigation of fraud at another branch, committed by a peon with the money deposited by the customers. The peon enjoyed a good reputation among all types of customers. It was a small rural branch. Customers gave cash to him to deposit in a savings or loan account, but he pocketed the money. A complaint stated that peon committed fraud in connivance with the Branch Manager. All the villagers were pointing the finger at the Manager. When I started the investigation next day, villagers were agitated against me. Also, they said I was hand in gloves with the manager. I called two/three persons inside the branch, and they told me that the inquiry should not be in the branch and the presence of the Branch Manager but outside the branch and in the presence of two /three persons nominated by them. I agreed with the conditions that they should arrange for sitting, and one branch staff member, other than the manager, will also be with me. They agreed, and I investigated while sitting in the village. All the customers concerned were arranged by the villagers for investigation. The investigation concluded in a week, and the report was submitted. The villagers were pleased because of our quick actions in the matter. But the report was a secret document. Only the statements of customers who suffered were recorded in the presence of villagers, and I also got witnessed these statements from them. The person committed the fraud, but the behavior of the Branch Manager was not suitable for the customers, and as such, they wanted to see him suffer. I requested the Regional Manager to transfer the BM, to which he agreed.

After more than five years in the audit department, in July 2007, I was promoted as Chief Manager despite only 60 vacancies in India and over 800 competitors. On promotion, I was relieved for Delhi Zone to work in Naroji Nagar, New Delhi Branch, as Incumbent in Charge, where I joined on 09.07.2007.

Take Aways

- **Field visits are essential to know the correct position of customers and securities, so always have field visits before making any decisions.**

CHAPTER 7

CHALLENGES OF METRO CITY

DELHI POSTING

Upon my promotion as Chief Manager, the prospect of shifting my family to Delhi was easy for me. It was a smooth transition after settling in Bathinda and my son completing his plus two in the same year. He even secured admission to B. Tech in Patiala, making the move to Delhi much more feasible.

After joining here, a house was taken on lease in the Dwarka area, about 20km from my office. One of my colleagues, Sh Sachdeva, helped me to settle in Delhi as the city was new to me and strange because I had never worked in any metro city before. Before joining the branch, I visited Delhi only twice, for one day each. My predecessor in the branch was also very helpful, and the entire staff was very cooperative. After a few days in the city, I never felt that this was a strange place for me. For about one month, I stayed alone in the vacant flat of my colleague and then finalized one flat on lease having an area of 900 sq. feet. The neighbor was a lovely family and was very cooperative. We shifted our household luggage on 1st August 2007.

At that time, I owned a Maruti Alto car, which I drove from Bathinda to Delhi for the first time along with family and relatives, but with great fear and pressure. We reached Delhi at 10 am, but by the time the household luggage was unloaded with the help of staff members. The flat had only two bedrooms, and everything was chosen according to the budget in metro cities. The flat was selected based on one of the critical factors: the good neighbors; when I went to see it, they offered me a cup of tea and had a lovely introduction. In metro cities, people have less time and are busy in their own world, but there was a difference here, so I decided to opt for that house. They were a perfect family who cared for us, and we have continued our friendship since then.

Now, my next task was to drive a car daily on the roads of Delhi in heavy rush and jams to reach the branch in time in time. I had no experience working in a metro city and driving a car on Delhi roads. I daily drove the car for three hours in a heavy rush using a clutch break race, a clutch break race, and it gave me sweats even in an AC car; anyhow, I managed it by having a pool with my other colleague, which gave me some relief.

The branch had a nice building owned by the bank, good business, and good staff. But the inside ambiance was not good. There was an incident of locker theft in the branch before my joining. As such, staff was terrified, and no outsider was allowed in the branch without valid reasons; there were several police and court cases because of locker theft. The branch's deposit was Rs. 60 Cr, and the advance was only Rs. 12 Cr. The tasks before me were to restore the confidence of staff and customers and improve ambiance and business growth. The need was also to restore customers' confidence because of the locker's theft case.

So, I started with the staff and customer meetings and met individually with high net worth customers. I suggested that the staff call a cleaning agency to clean the branch properly, but the staff was not ready because of locker issues. I made the decision, and two staff members were deputed to work with the agency people. Ultimately, there was some improvement in the ambiance of the branch. With all these efforts, the business started to improve.

HEAD OFFICE MEETING

The branch was near the Head Office building. In the Head Office, every Thursday at 9 am, the morning business meeting was conducted and chaired by the CMD. In the weekly meeting, two branches headed by chief managers were called from the Delhi Zone to attend the meeting with the Zonal Manager. Now, it was the turn of my branch, and I had to face the first time in my career, such a high level of meetings chaired by CMD and EDs, which comprised all General Managers. Before this business discussion, I had never seen the faces of such high-ranking bank officials. Now you can imagine what was running inside me. WAHAGURU SABDA BHALA KARE. As instructed with the necessary preparation, I reached head office at 8.30 am after parking my car with many fears and storms in my mind. With guidance from the guard staff, I entered the board room and sat on my seat behind my ZM. The meeting started as usual with a review of the Bank's and Zone's businesses. This was my first experience of such a high-profile meeting. Then my turn came, and the business of the branch was reviewed; with the grace of God, all replies to questions were given with confidence to the satisfaction of the Executive Directors, and commitment to business was also shown. The Executive Director asked me if I required any help from their side to achieve the budgets, and then I requested the renovation of the branch premises. It was immediately ordered to start the process. The review meeting ended on a positive note. I did not know any senior officers in the head office, but this meeting made me visible among all senior officers. After the meeting, many HO GMs complimented me for this good presentation.

The branch was renovated in the next 4-5 months. Splitting the staff's duties solved some operational problems, and the branch achieved all its targets in the December quarter and at the March year-end.

NEW CHALLENGES

One more experience I would like to share: there was a high-profile divorce case in Delhi court, and both the parties had a locker and account with the branch, and the high-profile bribery case account of Sibu Soren of JMM was also with the branch, for which the bank had produced many times bank record to the investigating agencies. In the divorce case, Branch received a court order from one party consisting of 3 family members, two advocates, and two police officers to open the other party's locker. There was a total mess in the branch. Now, I had to decide, and court orders were there, and the orders were to the extent of preparing the list of articles. I discussed the issue with my two managers, and they thought that we should also call our advocate for guidance. I agreed with the suggestion and called the bank's advocate in the branch. After going through the papers, he guided the branch by giving an opinion in writing. After taking all precautions as advised by the advocate, the party was allowed to operate the locker. Attending this type of high-profile customer was also a challenge. Both parties visited the branch on 4/5 occasions till all the issues relating to the bank were resolved. During their visit, I made good relations with both parties by providing prompt service and attending to them appropriately. A good chunk of government business was obtained from government offices, and the branch achieved all the budgets.

STATUTORY AUDIT

I got a telephone call from the branch's statutory auditors one Thursday, and they informed me that they would start the audit on Saturday. I told them that all the relevant papers would be kept ready. The branch was prepared for audit on the given day, but no one turned up. After waiting until 3 pm, I left the office. Only one manager was there doing some pending job. When I was about to reach home, I received a call from the auditor that they were reaching the office. After waiting, I explained that I had left the office, but they insisted on starting the job immediately. I returned and telephoned the loan manager and other related staff to report back. I reached back, meanwhile, other staff had also reached. The audit started, and at 8 o'clock, very little job was left. The auditor wanted to go and to finish it next day, but I requested that they complete the job the same night. He agreed, and the entire job was finished by 10.30 pm. All the staff had sigh of relief and had dinner with the audit team. So, the job was completed in 6 hours, which mostly take 4/5 days.

TRANSFER AND JOINING BRANCH PAHAR GANJ DELHI

In April, one Saturday, after completing the entire closing work, including audit work, I was coming to my hometown on leave for two days when I received a telephone call on the way that I had been transferred to branch Delhi Paharganj. There was a gap of three days in my relieving. During this time, I received many telephone calls from my well-wishers advising me to get the transfer order changed,as the branch was notorious for fraud, complaints, and many other bad things; I was also informed that there was a fraudulent account in the branch. Some of my friends even advised me to meet the Zonal Manager. After listening to all the views of my well-wishers, I thought that the branch had been there since 1942 and would be there in times to come. Someone else will be the Chief Manager, and if something terrible happens, it might occur anywhere, so I took the call to join there without hesitation and was relieved to join as Chief Manager at branch Pahar Ganj New Delhi. I was also advised to report to the Zonal Manager before joining the branch.

As per the advice, I reported to the Zonal Manager (Sh R K Dubey, the then General Manager, who later retired as CMD of Canara Bank). The meeting, which was not a mere formality but a comprehensive discussion that continued for about three hours, was about briefing the branch's critical issues. We delved into the branch's main problems, summarized below, demonstrating my dedication to addressing these issues.

1. There was a problem with customer service and customer complaints, and the main issue was that one customer, Mr. A, (name changed) on an average of 2/3 days a week, would stage a dharna at the main gate of the branch and raise many slogans against the bank and the staff. There were also many other complaints of service and complaints against my predecessor.

2. There was one fraud account of Rs 3 Cr, and I had to take all actions as per guidelines. Also, many accounts were about to slip to the NPA category financed by my predecessor.

3. Many proposals were pending, so I had to send my revised recommendations to the Zonal Office.

4. To reply to the inspection report of the branch, which has not been attended to for the last six months.

5. An average of 1500 customers were visiting the branch daily, and the challenge was to handle these customers so that the branch could function smoothly.

My predecessor and the manager credit were suspended, making it challenging to remove the irregularities they committed. Now, my routine had started handling these issues, and I will explain how these problems were solved or managed individually.

CUSTOMER SERVICE AND IMPROVEMENT IN WORKING

1. My first challenge was to handle the customer protesting at the branch gate on an average 2/3 days a week. After joining, I interacted with the staff about the customer and the other issues at the branch. Going through the discussions with the staff, I understood it was an ego issue for the branch management and the customer. The bank had to initiate the dialogue with the customer. So, I called the customer, but he was not ready to listen and even threatened me. He was a local leader and had the support of the public. I continued to contact him, and after 3/4 calls, he agreed to meet me. Even during a telephone call, I asked him if I could see him in his shop, but he refused to meet me. After continued efforts of 2/3 weeks, he came to the bank but not to my cabin. I went to the hall and requested him to join me for a cup of tea. Finally, he came to my chamber, and over a cup of tea, I had to listen to so many things about his past experiences. I assured him of the best service to the customers. He was not fighting for his interest but for improving general customer service in the branch, a second man and the Customer Care Officer were also part of the meeting.

I requested Mr. A that in order to improve the customer service in the branch he should give suggestions and out of his 10 suggestions, 4/5 were very valuable, and the branch was in a position to implement the same immediately. These were one additional cashier, one additional counter for passbook updating, availability of drinking water, and improvement of general customer service. I thanked him for his suggestions, and he assured me that we would implement these suggestions in stages. After the meeting, I discussed the issues with the branch officers and advised them to plan for the same, as these are precious suggestions. In the evening, a staff meeting was also held, and the entire staff was sensitized about the service on the counter.

Four/five suggestions were implemented in a week. The next time he visited the branch after two weeks and after seeing the changes he had suggested to improve customer service, he came to my chamber to say thanks. I assured him that I would extend the best service to the public. In stages, other suggestions that were worth implementing were also implemented. He was very much satisfied. After my joining, there was no dharna, no protest. Resultantly there was much improvement in customer service. He was the area's local leader, and he helped us with the opening of many good accounts. Now, he was the bank's ambassador. During my stay, there were no complaints of the branch regarding customer service.

What had I done? I only satisfied his ego. I listened to him and improved the branch's workings according to his suggestions, which were worth implementing.

When I was transferred from the branch, he visited the branch during a relieving party. He offered me a shirt as a token of love, but I refused. Then he said that he had stitched the same himself only for me and added, "Sir, this was a token of love and regard being younger brother because of your affection to the customers." Then I accepted the same. Till now, I have kept the shirt with a long story. I remember how I got it.

There were four receiving cashiers in the branch, and the average number of vouchers per cashier was 125 a day, so the cash book consisted of about 500 receiving vouchers per day. Daily in the evening, one or two vouchers needed to be searched out, resulting in the daily late closing of the cash and day-end activities. So, I called a meeting of concerned officials and introduced the system that the cashier would release vouchers in a bundle of ten vouchers in serial numbers. The bundle would be handed over to the cash book counter. With this simple improvement, all the problems were solved.

INSTALLATION OF ATM

Another instance is about one ATM working on the main gate of the branch. There always used to be a long queue of customers at that ATM. Daily cash withdrawal from the same was amounting to around Rs one crore app. Daily hits of the ATM were around 500 to 600. The ATM was number one in hits, availability, and cash disbursement in pan India. Given the rush, I was thinking of another ATM, but space was not readily available. Some space was available on the back side of the building under the stairs. The branch sent the proposal to the Zonal Office to install the ATM. However, the proposal was rejected because the space was insufficient. Branch officials and I revisited the place and created more space by shifting electrical panels to the other wall. I also arranged to fit wooden sheets on the wall to accommodate batteries and other accessories. Then, the branch again called the survey team. This time, they agreed, and with some strong recommendations, we got the sanction. The ATM was fully installed, and the inauguration was done by our Zonal Manager, who, after seeing the other ATM in the building, was very satisfied and asked me when this space was rejected earlier so how branch could get the approval now. Then, I told him about the efforts made by the branch to convince the team and to create more space within the given space. He commented, "The spirit is required everywhere; no job is impossible." So, with the functioning of this ATM, there was some relief on the front side of the ATM and improvement in customer service. Another ATM was functional in the main Bazar area to ease the rush. This successful ATM installation under challenging circumstances is a testament to our team's determination and problem-solving skills.

The average number of savings accounts opened in the branch was 20-25 daily. The officer working on this seat was very active. In the evening, we distributed three account opening forms each among staff members, and ATM and passbooks were issued instantly. At the end of the year, the branch was number one in opening savings fund accounts in India and got the cash award of Rs 50000, which the entire branch enjoyed by lunch. This achievement is a testament to our collective efforts and the dedication of our team to providing the best service to our customers.

working branch office NEW DELHI PAHARGANJ

HANDLING OF CUSTOMERS AND OUTSIDERS

To improve customer service, monthly staff meetings and quarterly customer meetings were conducted, thus solving the major issues. On average, 1500 customers visited the branch daily, and 25 accounts were opened on average daily. Four cashiers, two tellers, and two passbook counters were there, and despite that, there were always long queues on all seats until 4 p.m.

One more interesting incident happened in the branch. One day during lunchtime, when all the staff members were having lunch, and the guard was standing at the gate, two persons were trying to enter the branch, and the guard stopped them as it was lunchtime, but they pushed the guard and entered the branch. There was some minor physical clash among them, consequently, there were some injuries to both sides. Those two persons called the police, and the entire issue came to my chamber. The police wanted to arrest our guard, and I put forward all arguments that this was not fair as the guard was doing his duty and they were pushing the guard for entry into the branch during lunchtime, which was visible on CCTV. But the police were on the side of intruders and were seeking my permission to arrest the guard.Despite best efforts by the branch staff and me, they were not convinced, and at last, I agreed with one condition that an FIR from the bank side be also registered that two unknown people tried to enter the bank during lunchtime with the motive to loot the bank and our guard was also injured and as such, please take the necessary action. On listening to this from my side, within two minutes, all the police officers and both persons vanished from the scene.

In another case, during lunch hours, when the main gate was closed, one customer pushed the gate and our guard and entered the branch. Instead of waiting as the staff members were taking lunch, he started shouting in the hall. I was also having lunch in my cabin. I immediately came to the hall and requested the customer to sit in my cabin for 5 minutes. I told him to let me finish the lunch, and then he would be attended to. I also offered him a glass of water. He had to deposit a cheque for clearing. He was attended by the staff, but still, he was giving references to high-profile politicians and threatened to take action against us. After he left the office, I called the concerned officer and advised him to take CCTV footage of the incident and keep it safe with him as I was fearing some complaints. One day, a senior officer from the Zonal Office came to the branch to investigate the complaint after 3/4 days. The branch provided a copy of the CCTV footage and other information, and the complaint was closed.

DAV INSTITUTE MANAGEMENT COMMITTEE ACCOUNTS

The branch maintained all the accounts of DAV Institutes Management Committee HO at Delhi, and all transactions of all DAV schools and colleges with their head office were done through the branch. The bank charged commission for many transactions, cheque collections, and remittances as per guidelines. However, considering the account's value, the institution enjoyed all the facility at par. Every year before beginning, permission was obtained for at-par facilities. However, for the years 2007-08, it was not held on record, and all charges were debited to the account. Further, the following year, permission was off the record. Now, this was an issue for the branch. The branch was getting very pressing reminders from the Management Committee. I met with the secretary and assured him we would correct things in one month. Accordingly, we sent the proposal to ZO for refund of the charges earlier debited in the account and to allow us to continue chargeable transactions at par for the coming year. The branch got permission for the second recommendation but not for a refund of the charges. Again, the committee was very annoyed and pressed for a refund. The branch again recommended to ZO to refund the charges. After 15 days, we got permission to refund of 50%. The branch refunded the 50% charges and informed the committee, but again, they were unsatisfied. The branch again took up the issue with ZO, recommending a refund of the balance of 50% of the charges. This time, the branch got sanction for a refund of up to 75% charges. Now, the branch has refunded the further 25% charges and did not inform the committee; instead, we again took up with ZO firmly for permission for refund balance 25%. And finally, we got the permission. Accordingly, the committee was informed and satisfied. The branch got much help for the business from the committee. Afterwards I enquired from ZO why this issue was handled this way, whereas the permission could have been granted on the first or second recommendation, and I got the verbal reply that this was the only way to allow this.

NPA AND IRREGULAR ACCOUNTS

The other challenges were the NPA and irregular accounts in the branch. After my joining, a Chief Inspector reported to the branch to investigate all accounts financed during the period of my predecessor. In a way, it helped me to know the irregularities in the accounts. He took two months to complete the job, and the regular inspection was also completed during this time. The reports were bulky, containing 625 items, and the branch was rated high risk. This was another challenge for me, as I had to close the report and get the rating upgraded.

Two accounts could have been more troublesome. One was already declared as fraud, and follow-up actions were taken, while the other was a fraud but was not declared as a fraud account. The borrower was very clever. Whatever arguments we put up; all were negated by him. The Chief Inspector wanted to visit the properties mortgaged to the bank in the said account, however there was no support forthcoming from the party and the guarantor. As such, we could not identify the properties on site. So, I decided to get the properties verified through the Tehsildar and applied for the demarcation of the same, and the report came, which was different from the bank's record. Only the title deeds were there, but no property was on the ground, as stated in the title deeds. This was a solid reason to declare the account fraud, but still, the party insisted that he would mortgage new property and that the limit be renewed. However, I thought that the borrower was not trustworthy and may again play fraud, and it would be in the bank's interest to take necessary actions for recovery.

With the September closing looming, the pressure was on to prevent further NPA additions. Every document was at stake, ready to mark this account as NPA. The situation's urgency demanded immediate efforts to renew the account and steer it away from NPA status.

Meanwhile, the RBI inspection had started in the branch, and the RBI inspector discussed the account in detail with me, as all papers were in the file, and he instructed me to mark the account NPA immediately. As RBI inspectors have already declared the account NPA, it was marked as NPA. After half yearly of closing on 30th September, the branch took all recovery actions as warranted, such as a suit file and FIR with CBI as it was a fraud account. After two years, I saw the borrower in CBI court, where I was a witness, and he was accused.

Another account that was already declared fraud, I started to take all actions. The reason for the fraud of this account was fake title deeds. The branch issued notice to the borrower under the Securitization Act (although the title deeds were fake). On the due date, I took the symbolic possession of properties and published them in the newspaper as per rule, but the Zonal Office wanted to know from me as to how it could be done when the title deeds were fake. I took a firm stand and replied to the Zonal Office that I would not relinquish the charge unless otherwise advised by any court, and my documents are okay unless proven otherwise. In the meantime, a new development occurred, and Andhra Bank came forward and informed that the original title deeds were with them. So PNB and Andhra Bank both filed recovery suits, and, on our request, both cases were clubbed, and recoveries would be shared on the selling of properties. Meanwhile, the account was transferred to the recovery branch. Later, it was informed that all the properties were again fraudulently sold by the party to someone who also approached the court with a copy of the agreement to sell; after listening to all the parties, the court sold the properties to the same person, and the entire amount was deposited in court. It came to my notice that PNB recovered the principal amount in the fraud account. Thus, recovering the total fraud amount of Rs 2.92 crore app. (this development took place after my transfer from the branch)

In other accounts, much effort was made to recover or create a safety net for bank dues. During my period, many accounts were adjusted or regularised, thus saving the bank's money. The inspection report was also handled with much effort; every Saturday after lunch, the concerned staff used to sit in the office and remove the irregularities, and within 4/5 months, the branch was able to close the file, much to the relief of the branch and Zonal Office.

RECOVERY OF OTS AMOUNT

One NPA account in the branch had an outstanding amount of Rs. 4.60 crore against the limit of Rs 4 crore. The party was to appear before a committee of Executive Directors for a one-time settlement. Before the start of the meeting, I briefed the committee about the account and the security and the settlement should not be below the outstanding amount. Only penal interest could be waived. So, the settlement was approved accordingly but with the condition that payment should come in 3 months; otherwise, interest will be charged for the delayed period. But it took four months to adjust the account. The party sold his house, which was mortgaged with the bank. I took the information about the purchaser and opened her savings account with our branch for ease of transactions. A deposit of Rs 5 crore was received in our branch in the savings account, and the amount remained with the branch for one month. On the Registration date, the registering authority and the entire team came to the branch to register the transfer of titles. As there was a delay of 4 months, so the interest was chargeable over the OTS amount, which the party did not agree to. After settling all issues through ZO, there was a difference of Rs 50000. The party and ZO disagreed. It was 6 pm, and the registration authority requested that I should settle it. Then I took the call to waive Rs 50000. It was in the power of ZO, which had already declined. I took the call as the branch was recovering an NPA of Rs 4.60 crore, and 50000 was a small amount compared to that, and I wanted to take advantage of the recovery opportunity; otherwise, it would not come again. Then, all vouchers were passed, and the branch recovered an NPA of Rs 4.60 crore. All papers were released, and NOC was issued. Then I called the ZM to inform him about the recovery; he appreciated the same and also immediately enquired about Rs 50000. Then I replied that the branch also waived the same. Then he asked how the branch could do this when it was declined. I justified the same again, but he said I should pay the money from my pocket. I said I will do it. After some time, I again received a telephone call from ZM appreciating my action. He said he wanted to know whether CM was taking a decision; well done. The branch's action will be confirmed. Later, the same was confirmed.

VISIT OF ZM IN THE BRANCH

The branch was the number one pan India for opening savings fund accounts continuously for two years. The branch received an award of Rs 50,000 every year. One day our Zonal Manager visited the branch. He went through the entire work of the branch, and I offered a cup of tea to him; on my request, he took a cup of tea and told me that he took tea in a branch where he was satisfied with the working of the branch manager. I thanked him and said, sir and these were my best compliments. Then, he called his PA and advised that the CM's Performance Appraisal Report should be placed before him the next day. He was very much satisfied with the branch's work. One day, I visited the Zonal Office. ZM called me into his chamber and told me that 92 marks had been awarded to me in the PAR because of my performance. These are the highest numbers given to any Chief Manager. He also told me that I should continue to work with the same passion, and he assured me of the next promotion.

INCOME TAX DEPARTMENT ACCOUNT

One another branch, Jhandwalan Delhi, was merged with branch Pahar Ganj. This branch had a base of excellent customers of deposit and credit. A business of about Rs 70 crore was added in the branch business. One current account of the income tax department was also there. The department used this account to deposit money recovered in the search operation. The account was beneficial for the branch from a deposit point of view. It was the current account. The amount that was deposited remained in the current account for three months as a deposit, so the deposit and CASA target for March closing was not a challenge. This was also helpful in increasing the profit of the branch. I had excellent relations with senior officers of the department.

One day, one ACIT (Assistant Commissioner of Income Tax) requested sanction for a house loan to purchase a plot in one scheme of UP Govt in Noida (Yamuna Express highway). His wife was also ACIT (Assistant Commissioner of Income Tax). The plot cost was Rs. 47 lacs, and the loan required was Rs. 20 lacs only. Keeping in view the profile of officers, our business relations, and the eligibility of the borrower, the loan was sanctioned and disbursed in one day. When it was reported in the limit sanction statement, the branch received extreme observations, and I was also served with the tabular format for an explanation. However, as per the scheme, there was no problem with sanctioning the loan; the only issue was that the bank did not approve the project, and as such, its sanction was under the power of HO. I submitted the replies with justifications and reasons for sanctioning the loan and recommended confirmation of the action. However, the Zonal Office disagreed with me and insisted on adjusting the loan. Before going to the borrower with the request to adjust the loan account, I preferred to meet the Dy Zonal Manager and explain the entire story. I also informed them that the borrower is a high-profile officer and that all other conditions had been complied with. I sought his intervention to confirm the action. Further, the loan was fully secured, and there would be no problem in recovery. The Dy Zonal Manager called me after 3/4 days and informed me that the loan would continue and letters calling my comments would be withdrawn. I just had to submit the reply to the observations. So, the matter was got closed.

SHIFTING OF LOCKER CABINETS

Our branch housed approximately 3000 lockers, with many of them vacant. In a strategic move, it was decided to shift the locker cabinets with the lowest occupancy to other branches after relocating the occupied lockers to other cabinets within the branch. Two locker cabinets, with locker numbers totalling about 180, were made available for relocation to a rural branch on the city's outskirts. A meticulous process was followed, with all lockers being thoroughly checked along with the ledger account and two officers ensuring all lockers were vacant. With this careful planning and execution, both cabinets were successfully shifted, and the other branch was advised to send an officer to collect the locker keys. This process was a testament to our organization's commitment to efficient operations and customer service.

Meanwhile, a couple visited the branch on one Saturday to operate their locker, but it was unavailable. After a search, it was found that their locker had been shifted to one of the cabinets. It happened because their locker ledger sheet was placed by mistake in another ledger, which was a loose one. There were very anxious moments in the branch. I contacted the other branch and requested him to keep the branch open, informing him that an officer and a customer were coming to operate one locker that had been in one of the cabinets. The cabinets still needed to be placed in the strong room. The branch deputed one officer along with the customer to open the locker. They reached the rural branch at 2.30 pm. Both the cabinets were kept in the hall of the branch facing each other. The officer arranged some labour and separated the cabinets, and then the locker was operated. Thankfully, everything was intact. Then I received a telephone call from the concerned officer saying that what was needed had been done and the customer was satisfied. After that, I took my lunch.

The business and customer service of the branch improved a lot during the period of my incumbency. The branch was tough to handle; as many as 1500/2000 customers visited the branch daily. Another challenge was that petty thieves and fraudsters always roamed the branch because of the location, and we had to keep the customers on alert. Almost every day, strange incidents used to happen there because of the heavy rush of customers. We had to adopt a new formula and strategy daily to run the show. But the staff was friendly and cooperative, particularly the second man, Mr Vishnu, the Manager, Mr. Singh, Malhotra, Nanak Chand, Devinder Singh, Kalish, and many others.

PROMOTION AS AGM

In April 2010, there was a circular for promotion from a scale of 4 to a scale of 5, and I was eligible, so I appeared in a written test and interview and qualified. The result was declared, and I got the posting at the Shakespeare Sarani Kolkata branch. As a curiosity, the weekly figures were drawn from the system, and the deposits of the branch were Rs. 70 crores, and advances were Rs 800 crore. I checked the statistics two/ three times because, in the present branch, the credit figure was only Rs. 45 crores. Now, the challenge for me was handling the branch's credit portfolio, for which I needed to gain more knowledge of. I was relieved on 14.06.2010 and joined on 15.06.2010.

Take Aways

- **The spirit is required everywhere, no job is impossible**
- **Attend meetings of seniors with confidence and complete preparation and, with the right attitude**
- **Always cooperate with auditors and inspectors as they have to do their job.**
- **Handle customers with a calm mind and no ego. Please understand you are there because of the customers.**
- **Closing the inspection reports is very important in the career of a manager.**

CHAPTER 8

WORKING AT KOLKATA

JOINING AND BRANCH

Everything was new for me: the city, the state, the language, the working culture, the customers, etc. It seemed as if I had come to some foreign country. Although branch business figures were Rs. 900 crores, the inflow of customers was very thin, and staff was much more than required. Some clerks and officers had jobs of only 2 hours. It was a branch with an extensive credit portfolio, just like LCB, and the advanced portfolio was equal to LCB Kolkata. Big loan accounts of heavy industries like cement, iron, and power and accounts of Govt organizations like MSTC, CESC, and DVC (Damodar Valley Corporation Central govt company dealing in power having term loan Rs 300 crore) MSTC (Metallic Scrap Trading Corporation having limit of Rs 2200 crore) CESC (A big industrial house of Kolkata having responsibility of production, distribution of power in Kolkata).In the first two companies, the accounts were in multiple banking arrangements, and getting the limit availed was a challenge because of interest rate competition among banks. If any banks offer better rates, other bank accounts come to credit. CESC was a cash-rich company . 90% of the advance portfolio in value terms was in consortium arrangement. It was also a foreign exchange-authorized branch, and its share of the foreign exchange business in Circle's business was 80%, around Rs. 4000 crores. Its share of the total business was 40%. of the total business of Circle.

UNDERSTANDING OF CREDIT

Understanding the intricacies of credit, consortium arrangements, and the flow chart of all the industries was crucial. The Chief Manager, under whose tenure all these accounts had come to the branch's fold, was posted in the Circle Office and oversaw the credit portfolio, with most of the accounts being of HO sanction. However, as the branch head, I couldn't absolve myself from my responsibility. I needed to grasp these credit matters and make informed decisions.

Therefore, I called a meeting of all the staff working in the credit department. In the meeting, I admitted that although I am the branch's AGM, I only have a little knowledge of significant credit. I said that I require three months to understand and learn. Till then, I told them that I would need your cooperation. The staff was excellent and could handle the credit portfolio. They continued working on the same lines, and I started learning enormous credit. I started going through all the files, proposals, and sanction letters and also called the staff as and when any file was put up to me. The concerned manager would discuss it with me about the issue, guidelines and I also started going through the bank's relevant circulars and guidelines and wherever required I also discussed the matter with the staff and Chief Manager (credit) in Circle Office.

I also started discussing issues with the Circle Office, Head Office, and some colleagues exposed to these guidelines, including SK Malhan and Sh. KK Singla, and many others. This approach taught me a lot. After three months, I could have independent opinions on the loan proposals and parties and make operational decisions.

Now, the branch was in my total grip, and it also started to generate fresh business, resultantly, the branch started growing, and the branch made major contributions to Circle's business figures.

THE POSTING OF A NEW MANAGER IN THE BRANCH

During the transfer and posting of staff, a manager was posted in the branch, and the branch received the transfer orders, but the officer had still not joined. In the evening, all officer staff came to my chamber and requested the transfer order for the newly transferred manager be got changed. I enquired the reasons. Then they informed me that he was a very hostile union leader, and, at one time, he had turned the table of manager in a branch and would not contribute to business but rather create problems. I listened to their submission carefully and told them to let him join, and I would ensure things went well. On joining, he was allotted a job by an office order, and he was kept under surveillance and counselled occasionally. But he did not show any sign of improvement. Others were also complaining against him. He used to leave the office at 5 pm daily without any sign of responsibility. It was the month of March closing. Other staff was again watching him. I advised the other staff to wait till the completion of the audit work of the branch. However, there needs to be improvement in the work and attitude of that manager.

In April, when all closing-related work was completed, and I was free from all these pressures, one Saturday, I drafted a letter about his work and called his comments. After signing the letter, same was delivered to him, and I left the office as I was going to home town in Punjab for one week leave. At 9 pm, while waiting for the train at New Delhi railway station, I received a telephone call from that manager who was worried about the letter. I told him that I was going on leave, so he should prepare the reply and submit the same. I will look into it and review it after joining. He said on the telephone that even his wife and family were worried. After I had taken leave, when I joined the office, he immediately rushed to my cabin and requested to close the matter. He said that the reply had been handed over to the Chief Manager. The reply was very lengthy and included the account of every day he worked in the office. The Chief Manager was sitting with me, and I called the manager in my chamber. I asked him whether he wanted to close the matter. He replied yes, sir. I advised him that if he wanted to close, he should submit a reply expressing regret for his conduct and ensuring good conduct as a manager in the future. He immediately agreed and submitted the reply accordingly. As such, the matter was closed with advice to him to ensure good conduct, and he was cautioned to be careful, and the controlling office was also requested to keep his conduct under watch. After that, he improved his work and became faithful to the bank. He appeared in the interview for a promotion, and the branch helped him with the promotion and also his posting.

It is the will of management to improve the conduct of the employees. No matter how mighty a leader is, if management has determined to get work done for him, he will work.

RECOVERY IN WRITTEN-OFF NPA ACCOUNTS

There were large numbers of education loan accounts that were written off and were 10-12 years old. I studied the files of these loan accounts. Almost 90% accounts of students who had cleared their last exam from IIM Kolkata had an average outstanding loan amount of Rs 4-5 lac. All the students might have been well placed, and the package would have been one of the best. The outstanding amount was minimal, the only issue was contacting them. The branch engaged a recovery agency for the purpose.

The recovery agency prepared a database of their last mobile number and mail address. One more source was Facebook. So, the branch started to search through all these sources, and a recovery notice was also sent to their parent's address. Through these efforts, the branch could contact 60% of account holders. Accordingly, the recovery process started by telephone and by mail. Those contacted were well-paid, some were employed in the USA, UK, and Germany. They were also well-placed in many other places in India. Statements of accounts were also sent to all. With these efforts we recovered 70% of the written-off amount in two years. At that time, there was an incentive scheme for recovery in written-off accounts, and the branch got the award continuously for two years. Whatsoever incentive was paid to the branch was spent on picnics with families of all staff members.

I maintained good relations with all the credit customers, which helped us generate a lot of business from DVC, MSTC, and CESC.

INTERVIEW FOR PROMOTION TO DGM

On the date of my joining and on the date, I appeared for an interview of AGM to DGM, the comparative business figures of the branch was as follows.

Deposit   Rs. 80 Cr.to Rs. 400 Cr.

Advances   Rs. 800 Cr. to Rs. 2000 Cr.

(This growth happened as significant contributions came from DVC, MSTC, and CESC). Because of the excellent service we extended to them and our relations with them, they always preferred PNB over other banks.

Considering the quantum of business growth, the interview was smooth. The question asked was how the business had grown, and I gave a detailed answer about all the strategies and measures that my team and I had adopted. The interviewing committee was satisfied with my replies.

After the interview, one of the Executive Directors called me into his chamber, and I requested him for a posting in the northen side. He agreed, as I had already completed three years in Kolkata, and he had also conveyed his best wishes for the promotion.

On the same day, I came to my parent's house in Mansa from Delhi and told them that I would be posted on the northern side, and on my next visit, I would return with all my luggage. All were very happy. I returned from Mansa to Kolkata on Friday, i.e., 19th April 2013, and reached Kolkata at 11 am the next day, i.e., Saturday. In the evening, at 6 pm, when I was busy in my room, and my mobile was near my wife, a call came. My wife, who had picked up the call, said it was from MD Kamath sir. Before listening to the phone, I told my wife that I had been promoted to DGM. Then I took the call, and it was best wishes from the MD, who called up personally on my promotion. After that, I received so many calls from my well-wishers on my promotion, and the next day, some of my colleagues visited my home along with their families. It was around 1 pm when I received a call from my Zonal Manager, who informed me that I had been posted as Circle Head Kolkata, whereas I was waiting for the north India posting, but it was again an eastern area posting. I had to cheer myself up, thank God, and prepare mentally for the next assignment.

Take Aways

- **It is the will of the management to improve the conduct of employees and how mighty a leader is; if management has determined to get work done from him, he will work.**
- **Always be truthful about your knowledge to your juniors and seniors.**
- **Learning has no barrier of age, grade, or subject.**

CHAPTER 9
CIRCLE HEAD KOLKATA

JOINING AND STRATEGIES FOR BUSINESS

I joined as Circle Head (CH) on 22nd April 2013 in the Kolkata office. At that time, the circle consisted of 120 offices spread across four districts, and its total business was around Rs. 12000 crores.

As per existing arrangements, every AGM/CM was guardian for 20 branches regarding their issues and development. The Field General Manager's office was also on the same floor. Presently, this office is called the Zonal Manager's office. After my joining, CM (credit) and CM (planning) were transferred, and many others were moved due to yearly transfers and promotions. Almost all things were new for me. There is a difference between working as a Branch Manager and a Circle Head. As branch head, you have to manage 20 staff members. As CH you must manage 1,500 staff members, make administrative decisions, handle many HR issues and unions, and get the business done through the branches.

In Kolkata, unions were strong and had bargaining power even on petty issues. The prominent union was BEFI, which had more than 90% strength. First, I received a telephone call from them to have a meeting for which I consented, having no other option. The leaders came on the given date and time. I thought 3/4 of the staff would come, but there were 12 people. I was a little confused, however, I agreed to meet them. During the meeting, my strategy was to listen and offer a cup of tea as it was the first meeting. They talked about many issues, and the meeting continued for one hour, but at the end, one of the leaders said something threateningly (I thought that). But I could not consume this language. I told them that necessary cooperation would always be from this chair, but if something is wrong from your side, then no one will be spared. Anyhow, the meeting ended on a good note.

Then, I had to focus on business strategy, for which I took following steps.

Every branch and branch manager cannot perform; as such, we had to identify the business potential of branches and the performing manager who could be posted in these branches. An average of 40% of the branches and the managers perform automatically, and the next 40% would perform by pushing from the controlling office, and the rest, 15-20%, are hard nuts to crack for various reasons.

The follow-up and control of the branches were entrusted to senior officers in the Circle Office, a testament to their expertise and dedication. Each senior officer was tasked with overseeing 15-20 branches, demonstrating the trust placed in their abilities. It was also planned that review meetings of these branches would be conducted collaboratively, with the guardians of these branches present. At every meeting, there would be at most 30-35 managers, ensuring diverse perspectives. The sessions, lasting 3-4 hours, were designed to be efficient and productive. During this time, everyone had the opportunity to contribute to the agenda. The sessions would be conducted twice a quarter, providing ample opportunities for feedback and improvement. One at the beginning of the quarter and the other one month before the quarter's closing to review.

Every Monday, the senior officers would be in one of their command area branches to conduct a recovery camp.

As per HO guidelines, senior officers visited every branch according to a schedule. They ensured necessary follow-up so that no branch remained without a visit. A customer meeting was also conducted in every branch once every half-year.

A fortnightly meeting of all verticals in the Circle Office to review pending issues and discuss the problems coming directly from branches.

All the branches would be given yearly targets in each parameter, but these targets would be divided into small units for a short period to review.

Opening new branches in potential areas and closing the loss-making business stagnant and close proximity branches.

With the implementation of these strategies, we initiated a process of sensitizing the staff of the Circle Office and the branches. The results were not far behind, with positive outcomes emerging after one quarter. It was observed that in every quarter, Circle achieved three or four budgets, a testament to the effectiveness of our approach. As the Circle Head, I was fully committed to implementing the above strategy and ensuring follow-up with all the concerned officials, a dedication that contributed to our success.

VACANT LOCKERS: A CHALLENGE

Another major issue in the Circle was vacant lockers and rent in arrears. One branch had vacant lockers of around 11000, and rent in arrears was Rs 55 lac. There was a total mess in the branch concerning identifying vacant lockers, a list of lockers where rent was due, etc. This was a big challenge as I had to face GM at HO in various review meetings. As in the default list, our Circle was number one in pan India. Now, this problem required immediate action. I deputed two senior officers to the branch for one week, first to sort out the list of vacant lockers, lockers having rent in arrear, and other actions to be taken to identify the cabinets having minimum occupancy. After completion of this exercise, the following action points were agreed to.

1. Notices were issued where rent was in arrears, and the issue was resolved by breaking open the lockers.
2. The process of shifting lockers from cabinets where occupancy was low to other cabinets so that a cabinet can shifted at the point of need.
3. Searching for a savings account and locker holder's FDs, if any, to recover the rent.

The entire exercise was monitored by a Chief Manager from the Circle Office along with the Circle Head, and a system was established to review the progress fortnightly. After one year of action, the rent in arrears, and the number of vacant lockers also came down. Because many lockers were broken open and arrears were written off, locker cabinets were vacated and made available to other branches. The same were deleted from the branch system. Some cabinets were exchanged in buyback with Godrej.

Head Office authorities very well appreciated the action.

IMPLEMENTATION OF PRAGATI CONCEPT

The other major challenge was to start the Pragati branches in Kolkata, as the union was totally against the concept. In Pragati's concept, one passbook updating machine, one cash receipt machine, and one ATM were to be installed in the branch along with queue management and some other layout changes to ease the crowd of general customers and offer better customer service to valued clients. The concept was successful in the initial branch in the Circle, so the next target was eight more branches. The following proposed branch was B R B Road, which had the union's main office, and all leaders were sitting there; all machines were ready but nonstarter. Senior officers from HO/ZO/CO visited to pursue the branch to start, but it was useless. One day, I visited the branch and met with branch staff. During the meeting, one cashier said that if the cash receipt machine started working, no customer would come to him (cashier), and the bank would throw him out of the job. Then I tried to remove his misconception, but it was useless because they were working on the directions of their leaders.

There used to be quarterly meetings with unions to address the issues, if any, at the Circle level. In the next meeting, I took a stand that there would be no meeting till the start of the Pragati concept at B R B B Road Branch. Whatever the union could do, I was ready to face any consequences. Although there were good relations with the union, things could have been better on this issue. The next day, I received a call from the union. They proposed conducting the first union meeting, and the problem would be resolved within three days. As we were working in good understanding, I agreed to the same. The meeting was held, and I deliberately did not discuss the issue. After three days, I got the message that the work had started. In the meeting, the significant decisions of the Circle were discussed with unions for their input, such as opening new branches, closing of branches, renovating branches, and shifting thereof, etc. The transfers of clerical staff were also discussed to the extent of calling three choices, being a metro city, so that staff may be comfortable.

JOINING OF NEW CLERICAL STAFF

A batch of 40 new clerks joined in the Circle. First, they had to report to the training centre in Kolkata. Staff Union leaders insisted that their posting orders be issued after consultation with them. Still, I refused as postings would be done in rural branches with vacancies. Mr. NK Garg AGM was deputed to hand over the posting orders to the new joiners; out of 40, 20 refused to take the orders. He telephoned me at 6 pm about the development, and I advised him that all the pending orders should be placed on a notice board and that he should leave the office. At 7 pm, many union leaders rushed to my office, and I clarified that no orders would be changed. Then I left the office. Around 9 pm, I received a telephone call from one leader requesting a change of 2 orders, and I agreed with the condition that all others join first. After three days, when all joined, including the persons whose transfer orders were to be changed, the needful was done.

PUNCTUALITY IN BRANCHES AND COMPLAINTS

Three Punjabis occupied senior posts: Sh P K Sharma FGM, myself, and Sh S K Behal DGM. We also enjoyed our posting in Kolkata. There are many family activities and official functions for business once a week. PNB remained in the news in newspapers and local TV channels of the excellent work done by the bank.

The other two critical incidents during my posting were that once I visited a branch at 10 am on a surprise visit and found the branch was locked, and no staff was there. This incident, which could have significantly impacted the bank's reputation, was immediately addressed. I shifted the manager and called the CM (HR) to depute an officer to that branch. He made immediate arrangements. The manager and other staff reported at 10.15 am. They were asked about the reason for the late opening of the branch. Still, they failed to give any satisfactory reply, so the manager was immediately transferred, other staff were sent on leave, and action was initiated. The union condemned this action, but it was an excellent signal for other branches on punctuality.

In another case, one lady manager was doing an excellent job as the second man in a branch. When she completed her three-year stay at the branch, I transferred her to another branch near her residence. She joined the branch, and after 2/3 months, some customer complaints were received about her behaviour. She was counselled, and she assured of good behaviour. But again, after a month, there were more customer complaints about her behaviour. Then I visited the branch, and she was counselled, and the entire staff was also counselled. Again, there was a complaint about her services. Then, one lady Chief Manager was deputed to inquire into the matter. She visited the branch on a particular date, and again, another complaint was received from about 20 customers about her behaviour. Then, she was transferred immediately out of Kolkata to a rural branch. However, the union was protesting against her transfer and also threatening me about her likely mental condition after the transfer. I took the stand that the transfer would not be cancelled. She had to join or resign. After many days, she joined there. After joining, she came to my office with her two children and two union leaders. She pleaded for transfer to Kolkata to look after the children as her husband was not residing with her, and there was no other family member. The union leaders also requested the same. She also assured me that there would be no future complaints and that she had learned a lesson. On the grounds of the given circumstances, her case was reconsidered.

The Circle was at the top on the pan-India basis for the highest number of complaints about customer misbehaviour, which the bank takes very seriously. As Circle Head, I had to bear the same from HO. Now, I decided there would be an investigation if there were any complaints about misbehaviour, and the concerned employee would be transferred out of Kolkata, irrespective of their cadre. This decision, which reaffirms our commitment to excellent customer service, was well communicated to all the unions and staff. Two /three transfers were issued on this ground, although there was resistance from unions. However, I clarified that there would be no compromise regarding complaints. Although they agreed with me, they used to protest for the sake of protest, which I understood very well. The complaints on this ground were brought to zero, and HO appreciated our efforts.

A bizarre case of irresponsible behaviour of a manager in an AGM branch was brought to my notice. On the date of one half-yearly closing in the evening, when exercise was done about the business figures, the Circle was found to have achieved many budgets, and one of these was saving fund deposit. This information was shared with all the branches, and they were also advised that efforts should be made to restrict any withdrawal of any deposit of Rs 5 lac and above. Moreover, working hours at the bank were also closed when this advice was conveyed. The figure was Rs 2007 crore against the budget of Rs 2000 crore for savings deposits. When the next day's figures were checked, the savings deposit was down by Rs 20 crores, which was very strange. It shocked us, and we wondered how it had happened. Then an exercise was done to ascertain the reasons, and we noticed that an RTGS of Rs 20 crore was done in a branch at 7 pm in a govt. Account. After the inquiry, one manager who allowed RTGS of Rs 20 crore without the permission of the AGM of the branch and Circle office was identified. Although legally, as per bank rules, he had done his job on the day of closing, a manager should be sensitive to discuss such huge withdrawal with the branch's AGM or inform the higher authorities. So that efforts can be made to stop the withdrawal. This insensitivity is not tolerable, i.e., at a manager's level. He was also shifted outside Kolkata.

MERGER OF BRANCHES

The other issue was a merger of branch N S Road with BRBB Road, and this was happening for the first time in the history of Kolkata. The reason for shifting was that the branch was working in own building, but it was declared unsafe by the fire department of Kolkata Municipal Corporation. There were about 40 unauthorized occupants in the building. A notice was also given to all unauthorized occupants for vacating the building, although cases were already there against the unauthorized occupancy. So, considering the safety of staff and the assets, the decision was taken to merge the branch with the BRBB Road branch. However, the union opposed it, and a meeting was held with the majority union, and they were appraised of it. Our Circle staff was terrified of union actions as the union was threatening various actions, and Circle staff came to my chamber to request to postpone the merger. This action will likely result in the closing/merger of many branches in the coming days. If I failed, the central issue of loss-making stagnant branches would never be solved, so I advised the staff to go all out and come to my chamber only after the branch merger. The branch was merged on the due date, and there were protests from the union. After the protest, they came to my chamber, and I elaborated on the benefits of the merger to them and gave them the list of other branches to be merged. After many days, they agreed but with some suggestions. So, during my tenure, about seven branches were merged, which were loss-making and stagnant businesses, but more than that, new branches were opened on the city's outskirts with all the facilities. All work was done smoothly with the active participation of unions.

The N S Road branch building was closed with a notice that the building was unsafe. One other issue cropped up: the water supply to the unauthorized occupants. As the supply was inside the branch and the branch was closed, the water supply to the unauthorized occupants was stopped by default. There were many protests by the residents, and they even threatened me and FGM for the consequences. Despite the pressure, an FIR was lodged, and an order of 144 was taken within 100 meters of our office and the BRBB Road branch. The police advised FGM and me not to visit that area. There was much pressure from outside and political sides to restore the water supply. But I took the stand that if the bank allowed water supply from the bank's building, then the bank case would become weak in the court where eviction suits were filed. There was much pressure for many days, and in the end, KDA (Kolkata Development Authority) allowed water supply from the other side. The bank filed a protest note with KDA. However, the bank always had the stand that water supply would not be restored from the branch.

BUSINESS AND PLANNING

As I followed the strategy discussed above during my posting of two and a half years, the good results came as follows. These strategic decisions helped us overcome challenges and led to significant business growth, instilling confidence in our approach.

Total business increased from Rs. 12500 crores to Rs 18000 crores

Total deposit increased from Rs. 6500 crores to Rs. 9600 crores

Total advances increased from Rs 6000 crore to Rs 8400 crore.

In recovery, the Circle achieved the recovery targets, and the NPA terminal level of accounts with balance in less than Rs 50 lac. The figure was down by 20% based on the figure as of 31st March 2014.

The primary duty of the Circle Head was to develop a strategy for business growth, follow-up, and control, and to follow up on each significant issue and every action for recovery from his table, mainly accounts with balances more than Rs. 10 lac and accounts where action under the securitization act is required.

TRANSFER

Madam Usha, the new bank MD, joined on 14th August 2015. After around 15 days of her joining, I received a telephone call from the MD stating that I had been in Kolkata for more than five years, I was expected to perform better, and the performance of Kolkata Circle was not up to her satisfaction, and asked me to improve the performance. As MD had directly called me, it had some meaning in my favor or against me. Anyhow, I continued my work and focused on the September budgets. Again, a call was received from the MD on around 20th September with the same message. I was sure of my transfer and told my wife to wrap up the luggage as a transfer order would be issued. On 4th October, transfer orders were on the bank's website advising me to report to HO to work as Divisional Head of the General Services Division.

On 15th October, I was relieved from my duties. The relieving party was a unique event, with 4/5 union leaders in attendance, presenting me with flowers. They expressed that in the history of the Circle, it was the first time they had joined the party of the Circle Head, a testament to our mutual understanding and respect.

Take Aways

- **Understanding the people working under you is most important for business.**
- **Follow-up is critical for success.**
- **Stick to your decisions if these have long-term effects on the growth of the business**
- **Always be punctual and disciplined so that your juniors may follow you.**
- **Do not tolerate wrongdoings and practices**

CHAPTER 10

WORKING AS DIVISIONAL HEAD IN HO

JOINING AND CHALLENGES AHEAD

I joined HO on 18TH October 2015. It was my first posting in the Corporate Office. First, I had to understand the workings of the Head Office and the Division; my boss was Mr M K Pangtey, GM. Most of the GMs and other senior officers were known to me. I met the all Executive Directors and General Managers. I also met the MD, who told me that my GM and I were posted to complete some particular tasks, i.e., the construction of the HO building. The job in the division was different from routine banking as it involved the civil, electrical, mechanical engineering, tender process, and services to the staff about providing infrastructure for office work and making the stay of senior officers comfortable at their residences, cars, telephones, etc. The primary issue was that everyone wanted the facilities, but the division had to follow the entitlements of the concerned officer as per bank guidelines. As such, sometimes some proposals were declined, so the division needed a better name among the staff working in the Head office.

On my joining, I reviewed all issues of the division and, after meeting with staff, advised them to follow the bank guidelines for entitlements but help out the staff and try how we could help them within the given rules instead of declining the issue. I also initiated a fortnightly review of pending issues with the division's CMs. Now, things started to move as it was clear that officers would be asked about the pendency after every fortnight. The major issues were -

The Head Office building at Dwarka was to be completed and which was under construction.

The renovation of bank flats was meant for senior officers which were in terrible condition.

Old cars have been dumped in buildings for the last ten years.

Many other projects were waiting to start.

Satisfaction of bank general managers with their cars, flats, and cabins.

Maintenance and up-keeping of HO building

To keep the morale high of the division staff, senior officers of other divisions sometimes rebuke the staff on petty issues. Staff feel very offended without any fault.

There were many other issues, but the above were the main ones I had to handle.

COMPLETION OF HEAD OFFICE BUILDING DWARKA

The major project was the completion of the HO building. The MD monitored the progress from her table. The project was behind schedule, and progress was not satisfactory. The CPWD was the executing agency; the contractors were M/S Ahluwalia Construction Company and M/S GODREJ.

There were already in place the fortnightly meetings at the site of all stakeholders to review the project, and some of the suggestions (regarding some changes in concept) discussed in the meetings remained pending for want of sanctions of the competent authority, which delayed the project. Our team worked on the approvals of bank-level issues so that the same may be expedited to CPWD and then to the contractor for execution. The problem of approvals was discussed with the MD, as it was one of the reasons for the delay. Bank had deputed two engineers to the on-site CPWD office to handle the project from all angles.

At the senior level, for follow-up, issues were discussed with top CPWD authorities and the director of M/S Ahluwalia Construction Company through meetings and various letters even to the ministry.

The project was geared up when our MD started to Chair the monthly review meetings. In March 2016, the project was in full swing. The tenders for furnishing for the top executive floor were also floated. This job was allotted to M/S Godrej. Some other small jobs were allotted, and during various meetings, the deadline was fixed to complete the project by December 2016. The review meetings were conducted fortnightly to review the work so that stakeholders who still needed to meet expectations were pulled up. After discussion with our MD, the decision was taken to give approvals at the division level on the issues on the bank's behalf, whatever was required in the meeting itself, and not to seek any prior approval from the MD. Still, the division had to give MD a note for information. With this decision, many things were clarified to CPWD in time, and the project started to show progress. The MD was pushing the project with keen interest as she was involved in the project from the very beginning when she was the bank's ED.

The expectations of MD were very high to complete the project by October 2016, and even in one meeting in July 2016, she desired to start working from the new building from 1st November 2016. Our GM, along with me, was under severe pressure. We both returned to the office after the meeting to find out the solution and how to inform the madam that the project would be completed in June 2017. As CPWD was a central government institution, many compliances were to be made to reply to the CVC in future inspections by CVC. So, things cannot be rushed with blind eyes, keeping in view the compliances and quality. In the chamber of our GM, a meeting of all senior officers relating to the project was held to discuss how to bring to the MD's notice that the project would be completed after June 2017. As such, the MD cannot start working from there before that. Even the MD needed more time to be ready to listen to the CPWD senior officers. We decided to write to the Secretary of the Ministry of Works. So, one DO letter from the table of our GM was written to the Secretary. Then, the secretary reviewed the entire project with CPWD. Although the bank was not a party to that review meeting, but every progress made on the subject was in bank's notice.

In September, the bank received a reply to the letter from the secretary informing that the project had been reviewed with CPWD and would be completed by June 2017. This news was met with a sigh of relief, marking a significant milestone in the project's journey. The MD's agreement to the same further solidified the sense of accomplishment. Despite the pressure from senior colleagues, the team remained focused on the project's successful completion.

Almost nine months were there, and the next major issue before the division was to put in place various agencies for the maintenance of the building, canteen services, mess services, horticulture, etc.

It was the duty of the division. So, multiple teams were formed in the division to visit various such buildings. Many MNC buildings, airports, 5-star hotels, and some govt buildings were visited to know the materials used, workforce requirements, and the level of standards in the tender. The same exercise was done for the canteen, mess, and other services.

Accordingly, tenders were floated well in time, and service providers for all these facilities were in place before the scheduled completion date. I record the contribution of Sh Sonny Paul, Sh K K Aggarwal, the then both AGMs and Sh Neeraj Kumar, Sh Lalit Kumar, and Sh Prabhat Shukla, CMs and many junior colleagues. The project was going on per the revised schedule and was to be completed by 30th June 2017. In May, there was a change of MD of the bank, and a new MD joined. A presentation on the project's status was made to the new MD, Sh Sunil Mehta, and the new MD instructed that there should be no haste and that the project should be completed satisfactorily.

In June, our GM, Sh Pangtey Ji, retired, but by then, the project was almost complete; some final touches were going on, and we were waiting for statutory clearances from different departments. By August 2017, all clearances had been received and We decided to shift at the earliest. The number of employees was counted per division, and also the seating capacity of each of floor was determined. The idea was to accommodate each division on one floor; the other was how many divisions frequently visiting the TOP management. Those divisions will be accommodated on the 5th and 4th floors, and divisions, where the maximum number of outsiders and vendors are visiting, will be accommodated on the ground and first floors. Accordingly, MD&CEO approved the sitting plan of the divisions in the new building.

SHIFTING TO NEW BUILDING.

A tender was also floated for mover and packers to shift records of different divisions to the new building. In the first week of September, when moving and inauguration of the building were discussed with MD, it was decided that time should be sought from the finance minister for inauguration. The GAD division was advised to shift first to see the necessary arrangements. The division reviewed the readiness of each floor accordingly, and dates were fixed for the shifting of each division. Packers, the concerned division, and the technical staff of our division, contractor, and CPWD were on the same line for hassle-free shifting, and every division was notified of the date of shifting in advance for their readiness. The entire exercise was to be completed in 6 days.

A chart containing the name of the division was prepared in our division. The shift date and the floor on which the division will shift were circulated to all divisional heads, vendors, packers, movers, and CPWD teams. There was also another exercise in our division; teams of four persons were on standby, including a civil engineer, an electrical engineer, one member from the sitting plan committee, and one from the maintenance committee. These teams were also informed about the shifting plan. These teams' duty was to prepare the floor before shifting of any division. So, the entire shifting exercise was completed in 6 days without any hassles. The planning and shifting was very much appreciated from all corners.

The date of inauguration was fixed at 6 November. With efficient time management, we started the shifting on 22 October and completed it by 29 October 2017. The GAD Team was also busy preparing for the inaugural function. The entire road map was prepared. Six committees of GMs arranged the inaugural function, and ED headed them. However, MD and ED gave the overall responsibility to our team, showcasing our division's productivity and effectiveness.

Formal permission for shifting was even obtained after the exercise was completed. Authorities were pleased with how the shifting was done without wasting workforce days.

For the inaugural function, different committees were formed and headed by GMs, but GAD had overall responsibility. Two things were essential and required for the inauguration, i.e., a bust of LALA LAJPAT RAI JI has to be in place, and the other the inauguration name plate. The order was placed, but we needed clarification about the supply, and both issues disturbed the division. However, I took a proactive approach and placed an order with another vendor as a backup plan. This demonstrated our division's problem-solving skills and preparedness. Fortunately, both orders were received in time, ensuring a smooth inauguration.

Two times, a dummy exercise was done for the function along with the MD and CEO, and any shortcomings were taken care of. The function was a great success, and the bank acknowledged and received appreciation from all corners. It also received good publicity.

TAKING POSSESSION OF THE GURGAON PLOT

There was a plot in Gurgaon in the name of a bank allotted by HUDA. The size of the plot was three and a half acres approx. The plot was allotted in 1986 under the name New Bank of India. After the merger of NBI with PNB, the plot became PNB's property. There was a lot of correspondence with HUDA on the physical and paper possession of the plot. Some individuals also had disputes regarding this property, which was part of the plot. Before our joining, Sh G S Chouhan, former GSAD GM, had solved this issue. But paper possession and title deed were not there. The follow-up was started. The dealing officer in HUDA was very hostile. Despite our best follow-up and taking up the matter with their HO, there was no movement. We even started to depute one officer to HUDA daily to sit there, and I also started to visit the office twice a week. He always promised but put off for one reason or another. After a follow-up of six months, the division decided to meet the Administrator of HUDA Gurgaon. Our GM and I met the Administrator, a very young and active officer. We told him the whole story of the plot possession, and he promised to get the things done in 30 days. He called the dealing officer and other staff and instructed them to complete the process in 30 days.

Accordingly, we waited for not 30 days but 45 days. After that, an officer was deputed to know the fate, but to our surprise, there was no movement in the file. I again discussed the issue with the General Manager and decided to meet the administrator again. After a prior appointment, we both met him in the office. While listening to us, he was also shocked and requested that we sit in the waiting room. He called the entire staff and advised them to go to their seats and prepare the note and letter to be given today. All the dealing staff were in his cabin, and he urged them to sign there. After one hour, we got the letter of possession, and after that, the rest of the registration formalities were done in 30 days. Bank became the absolute owner of 3 ½ acre plots and could proceed with any development activity. Presently, the bank is constructing data centre there.

PROMOTION AND TRANSFER

As I was a candidate for the promotion from DGM to GM, the successful shifting of the HO building and the excellent opening ceremony made me a more deserving candidate. General Manager GSAD Mr. Gandokh retired on 28th February 2018. On 1st March 2018, the bank issued an office order in my name to work as GM GSAD (officiating), which happened without any interview. I was also told that it had happened for the 1st time when staff had been given the next grade assignment without an interview. Therefore, my regular promotion was almost assured (in my opinion). The interview was held on 25th March, results were declared on 31st March, and I was declared successful.

The promotion theory is prominent (my personal view): For a Scale of 1 to 3, what do you know? for scales 4 and 5, to whom do you know? For scale of 5 and above, who knows you?

On promotion, I was posted in Zonal Office Agra for taking charge of Zone as Zonal Manager on 1st August 2018.

Take Aways

- **Decision-making always plays a significant role in completing a job on time.**
- **Systematic and timely follow-up is required to break challenging nut issues.**
- **Well planned, half done.**

CHAPTER 11

WORKING AS ZONAL MANAGER AGRA

JOINING AND CITY

Agra is a historical city with the Taj Mahal, one of the world's seven wonders, the fort of the Mughals, and Gurudwara Guru Ka Tal, having memories of four Sikh Gurus who had visited the place. Agra was the next place after Delhi for the residents and Darbars of the Mughals. The other essential places near Agra were Krishan Janam Bhumi Mathura, Brindavan, Dwarka, Fort of Gwalior, and Fatehpur Sikri. The other important thing about Agra is the well-known sweet item Petah, which is famous for its unique taste and variety. The Agra leather industry also has its name and fame. Milk and its products and edible oil are other famous items.

I joined Agra on 26th April 2018 and worked as DGM, second man for three months. These three months helped me understand the Zone and its workings and circles. My predecessor, Sh P K Shrimal retired on 31st July 2018. So, my promotion was released on 1st August, when I took charge. On 1st August, I started working as the Zonal Manager of the Agra zone.

One day before I took charge when the office was preparing for the retirement party of my predecessor, Sh P.K. Shrimal ji, at around

5 pm, two workers' union leaders entered my cabin and started talking loudly. I could not understand the reason. Then, without going into the issue, I handled them firmly and advised them to go out, and if they wanted to discuss any issue, they can take a prior appointment, and after that, they went away. I analysed the problem and felt that they wanted to impress me as the award staff leader, but I showed them who the leader was. Anyhow, they never visited my office during my tenure. If there were any issues, they only requested by telephone.

I joined Agra on 26th April, so I had time to understand the Zone before taking charge on 1st August. There was a good scope of business, but the ticket size was small, which was to be attended to at the branch level and the Circle level, so the role of the Zonal Office was to monitor and follow up and hand-holding of Circles Head and branches. The other analysis I did was that there were 54 Chief Manager branches, and their business share was around 60% of the total business of the zone. If these branches started to perform, then the buisness would automatically grow.

BUSINESS STRATEGIES

So, I adopted the following strategies.

1. The Zonal Office will directly monitor the Business of all Chief Manager branches. The Zonal Office and the Circle will control these branches for business purposes.

2. All Chief Manager branches would send weekly reports to ZO every Monday on selected parameters such as the opening of savings and current accounts, recovery, loan-sanctioned, third-party business, etc. The reports were put up before the Zonal Manager every week, fortnightly, and monthly on a consolidated basis

3. Review meetings were held with all CM branches based on their monthly reports.
    The system is that when you ask someone about business regularly, the person will start to perform.

4. All other branches are to be followed up by Circles Heads on the same lines.

5. There should be competition among Circles about the business for achieving targets and for the number of accounts opened recovery made, loans sanctioned under different parameters, third-party products, and branches participating in each parameter.

6. Each branch to contribute in respect each parameter of the business.

7. Awareness about business done on the previous day by the Circles under the selected parameters; this was the duty of the Zonal Office to share with Circles early the next morning. Each department is to share the previous day's progress with the Circles Head WhatsApp group on all parameters at 9.30 am daily, along with cash holding of the Circles so that steps can be taken to shift excess cash to the currency chest.

8. The Circles were proactive in their approach. They were given daily recovery targets as per NPA figures, which were closely followed up and monitored. This demonstrated the team's commitment towards meeting these targets.

The follow-up on the above guidance was established in two months. Now, the roles of the Zonal Office and Circles staff were already defined, and they started working on these lines for follow-up. The Zonal Office, as a crucial guiding and supporting entity, ensures that we all work towards our common goals.

There were five Circles consisting of 29 districts of Uttar Pradesh: Agra, Bulandshar, Jhansi, Moradabad, and Bareilly. All five Circle Heads, known for their diligence, and the second man of the Zonal Office, Mr. Wahi, who was also very responsive, hardworking, and reliable, formed a fantastic team. With six DGMs, it was a tremendous team to move further. Their hard work and dedication were instrumental in our success.

BUSINESS PERFORMANCE

Under the guidance of the Circles Head and the support of the Zonal Office, Zone Agra consistently excelled in recovery, the opening of saving accounts, recovery of locker rent, and other campaigns run by the Head Office. This was not a stroke of luck but a result of our collective efforts and strategic planning. Zone Agra maintained its position at number 1 or 2 on all India basis in a maximum number of parameters throughout all the eight quarters of my tenure as ZM. This is a testament to our collective success, and I am proud to have participated. I will only mention the following discussions held in HO meetings.

1. All other Zones were asking me how the performance was coming. What is the strategy of Zone?
2. In one of the meetings on 1st January 2019, the MD and CEO asked me what the resolution of the Zone of New Year would be. I replied that I would resolve that "each branch contributing to each business parameter." Then the MD said that was his takeaway. This was very encouraging for me.
3. In another review meeting, the MD told other HO GMs that he was satisfied with the performance of Agra Zone and would not ask anything, but GMs may discuss any issue they want. However, GMs reviewed the performance. The meeting ended, and I got great encouragement again.

I was consistently acknowledged in almost all meetings for various reasons, and Agra Zone was recognized for its outstanding business performance.

The strategy we implemented during my tenure was a collective effort, with all Circle Heads and branch staff responding positively and working hard. Each branch and every staff member contributed their best for the organization. Our performance was a testament to the power of teamwork and the dedication of each member of the staff.

PROMOTION

After two years of stay, in March 2020, the promotion process started and many promotions happened in all grades in the Zone. Four chief managers were promoted as AGM, and out of six DGMs, three were promoted as GMs comparatively in a small zone due to good performance. Due to the merger of three banks, Govt of India created a new post of CGM in all the banks having business more than Rs. 10 lac crores. The ratio was that for every four GMs there should be one CGM in grade 8. I also appeared for interview for CGM which was held on 22nd March 2020 for ten posts for 2019-20 only. But I could not get through it. I felt a little surprised, as I was the performing Zonal Manager, and I wondered why I had been ignored. This disappointed me, Perhaps I was straightforward because of my rural background, or possibly my not-very-polished delivery of words had not gone well with the interview board. However, there was another opportunity in April as an interview was held on 18th April for vacancies for 20-21. Before the interview board, I explained my performance in the Zone, and a few questions were asked.

On 20th April at around five o 'clock I received a telephone call from our MD&CEO. On seeing his number on my mobile,

I was delighted that this call was probably to inform me of my success in the interview. It is customary in the bank that before the official declaration of the result, the candidates were informed about the success by the MD&CEO for promotion to the top post. He conveyed his blessings on my success in promotion as Chief General Manager Grade 8 from 1st July 2020. This was a great success for me as only four persons were promoted from the field out of 19 candidates; the other three were ZM Mumbai, ZM Delhi, and ZM Kolkata. I was in ZM Agra, which is a relatively smaller zone. The promotion was performance-based. The size of your business unit does not matter in promotions—your performance matters.

DISCIPLINARY ACTIONS

When I was posted as Zonal Manager and Circle Head, I also performed the role of disciplinary authority. While performing that role, I kept one thing in mind: not to make a hasty decision to complete the files, and I used to review all the relevant records thoroughly. In one of the cases in Circle Office Kolkata, the file remained on my table for about two months despite pressures to clear it fast. It was a duly recommended case against some senior officers. I was unconvinced and believed that whatever happened, the concerned officers had worked in the bank's best interest. So, taking some clue from the record, I recommended dropping of the cases (After continuously thinking about the issue for two months). It was a pleasure that HO, too, agreed with my recommendations.

In another instance at the Zonal Office Agra, a scale one officer approached me with a severe issue. He informed me that he had been served with a charge sheet under major vigilance, even though he had not recommended or sanctioned the particular case. He had merely opened the loan account in CBS. I carefully reviewed the records and verified his claims. Upon finding his statements true, I recommended that the HO vigilance division drop the charge sheet. I am pleased to share that the Chief Vigilance Officer (CVO) agreed with my recommendations, further affirming the bank's commitment to fair and just practices.

When confronted with a highly intricate case involving a senior manager, I meticulously scrutinized a 15-page tabular record of all the irregularities. After issuing the concerned officer a tabular of the outstanding irregularities, there was a system in the bank to close the inspection reports by issuing tabular to the concerned officer. Despite the successor's lack of diligence, I remained resolute in my decision to resolving the outstanding issues. Before taking a final decision, I instructed the Circle Head for formation of a team of 3/4 officers, including the present and the past incumbent, to ractify the irregularities. The Circle Head heeded my advice, and after a week, the team resolved all irregularities except 2/3, and the tabular was dropped. I then initiated a DA case against the branch's incumbent, who had failed to handle the inspection report. This case is a testament to my problem-solving skills and unwavering commitment to ensuring efficient and effective resolution of complex issues.

In a highly time-critical case, an officer was on the verge of retirement, and just a week before his retirement date, the case was sent to the vigilance department HO for first stage advice. Recognizing the pressing nature of the situation, I promptly reached out to the CVO and presented the case. His immediate decision enabled the case to be resolved a day before the officer's retirement, relieving him of undue stress. This swift and responsible handling of a high-pressure situation underscores my commitment to efficient and effective problem-solving.

TRANSFER TO DELHI

Due to Covid 19, there was a lockdown in the country, and fear was very high during the pandemic; there was no movement from one city to another, and all movements were closed. You had to get permission from DM to move from one town to another. Even our drivers did not attend to our duties, and we had to our own cars. On 13th May 2020, I received a telephone call from the Executive Director advising me to report to HO Delhi immediately. I was very much in a fix keeping in view the pandemic. I was relieved on 16th May 2020 and planned to go to Delhi. I got permission from DM due to official exigency. I requested the GM GSAD for one accommodation till I do not shift my luggage. The bank was kind enough to help me. So, I moved to Delhi to join my new assignment.

Take Aways

- **Each branch to contributes to each parameter of the business.**

CHAPTER 12

CGM IN HEAD OFFICE

JOINING

I reported to the HO on 18th May 2020 for my further duties. I was posted as Head of GSAD, Rajbhasha, Security, Printing, and Stationary. The MD&CEO, and four EDs advised me to settle all the department issues arising from the amalgamation of three banks. I was also assured of support from the management wherever required within guidelines. On 1st April, two other banks, OBC and UBI, were merged with PNB. My predecessor was going to retire on 31st May 2020.

Now, I had prepared list of the issues to be settled first.

1. An exercise was to be done for the seating plan of all the divisions of the HO, which was spread across different buildings in Gurgaon, Kolkata, and Delhi. Each division worked in solo from all places.

2. As per the new structure plan, new Zonal offices, Circle Offices, RAPCs, and MCCs will be opened at different places in a time-bound manner.

3. Allocation of space to these offices where space was available in own buildings or lease buildings.

4. Utilization plan of bank's buildings, pan India city wise, and identifying surplus, if any, for sale.

5. Merger of branches and guidelines thereof for the same.

These were the critical issues because of the merger besides the routine job of the division.

PLANNING AND EXECUTION

To handle all these jobs, the division should have sufficient staff. Accordingly, after a discussion with Mr Arora, the then GM in GSAD from EUBI, who was very intelligent, humble, and had excellent relations with staff, prepared the list of staff working in the field. CGM HR was requested that those persons in the division be posted as a team to be built up to complete the essential jobs. HR was so helpful that all eligible staff were posted. Mr Rajesh Arora, GM, was very competent, and I could trust him to any extent. Although presently, he is not among us. He always stood with me, and his valuable input could not be ignored.

The next task was to have a fresh duty sheet in the division, with the allocation of the above five tasks. A team of two DGMs, one CM, and two senior managers could complete the duty sheet job in a week. The duty sheet was ready to be implemented in 15 days. The division was divided into three verticals consisting of tasks numbers 1,3 &4, and 2 &5, and the third vertical to look into other issues such as cars, flats, and other expenditures. DGMs headed all the verticals and were advised to draw up their plan for the jobs allocated to them. When plans were ready, we had to follow up for execution.

After discussion with other stakeholders, a plan was prepared to allocate space to various divisions in the HO building consisting of the Dwarka Building and the Gurgaon Building. With the permission of the competent authority, a note was circulated to all concerned for shifting, and our team was ready to assist and help in the process smooth shifting. Many issues in this exercise were resolved with persuasion or requesting (keeping in view the institution's interest) where resistance was more. Even when one division was shifting from one floor to another in the same building, there was a lot of resistance without any reason. Tactfully, it was kept pending, and the rest of the jobs were completed. Now, the issue of shifting one division was there, which I had personally discussed with the concerned CGM and GM. After I handled the problem, it was settled. The concerned vertical head resolved all other issues. In 60 days, all HO divisions worked smoothly from their respective new places, and all seniors appreciated the efforts.

Another issue was the top management officers' use of the bank's cars. It was the division's duty to implement the policies in each area. One top management official on transfer from A place to B place requested by going on bank's car and was allowed. He was also allotted another car of his entitlement at his place of posting but he refused to return the car of place A, where he was earlier posted. The vehicle was returned with the follow-up and with the intervention Executive Director. Later on, the officer was posted in HO on the higher post, and one day, he expressed his displeasure to me about the issue. But I replied that I had decided based on the bank's policy.

Then, guidelines about utilizing bank buildings and merging of branches were circulated to the field staff. Now, it was a matter of following up with the field.

MERGER OF BRANCHES & OTHER ISSUES OF FIELD

For the other issues, we made our agenda paper and strategy for the field to work on these papers, such as the merger of branches. All branches within a 200-metre distance, business stagnation, loss-making, and businesses less than Rs. 10 crores were eligible for the merger. The maximum area required for a particular office was defined through a policy duly approved by the board for optimum building area utilization. Wherever owned buildings were available, it was decided that all back offices should be shifted to these owned buildings and that back-office buildings should be surrendered to save rent. After this exercise to identify the surplus or additional area, field functionaries were allowed to open new offices in freshly hired areas.

The next plan was to follow up on the above strategy with the field. All 24 Zones were divided into six groups, and in the first week of every month, a VC was conducted with all DZMs, the Circles Head, and the concerned staff. Every issue was discussed, and necessary guidance was provided to the field. The performance of each Zone was also discussed, and the following, way forward was also decided. The agenda of the meetings was mainly the utilization of buildings, merger of branches, and follow-up action after mergers, i.e., date of merger, surrender of building, use of strong room gate, shifting of lockers, etc, change of sign boards, and other issues. The merger of branches was based on within a distance of 200 in the metro area and 500 meters in another location, and there would be only one branch in a village, and loss-making branches and stagnant branches too to be merged.

The Video Conferences were held with all Zones and Circle Heads every month to monitor the progress of each Circle. The Circles that did not reach the desired level were pulled up, and results started coming after 2/3 meetings. The purpose of these meetings was to sensitize the staff in the field about the expectations of the corporate office, as the corporate office was answerable to GOI to get the maximum benefit from the merger of banks. As a result of these meetings, the division identified the surplus properties for sale and the merger of branches to save on operational costs and rent.

In one of the DFS review meetings, our MD&CEO committed to merging 500 branches by March 2021. As such, this was the division's target. At the end of March 2021, approval was given for the merger of more than 500 branches, several proposals were in the pipeline, and a good scope was there for the merger of more branches. One day, MD called me and congratulated the team for the merger of 500 branches and also asked the way forward as I had the idea of the scope of the merger. I therefore committed to merge a further 500 branches in 21-22. The next day, there was a press conference because of the bank's annual results, and the MD announced before the press that PNB would merge a further 500 branches in the years 21-22 to get the maximum benefit of the merger.

The next day, it was a headline in almost all newspapers, so it put more responsibility on the Division to perform. The team was fully charged and committed to fulfilling this target. One DGM, 4CMs, one senior manager, and another scale 1-2 officers were very active in the branch merger section. Head Office Building Committee meetings were scheduled fortnightly, and 30-40 proposals were placed in each meeting. Each Circle was monitored monthly, and the target of further 500 branches was achieved on 30th March 2022, one day before my retirement. Many buildings were identified as surplus in India after optimum utilization of the area, and some were sold out. All new offices were opened in a time-bound manner.

NEW POLICIES AND POWER CHARTS

The following vital policies were drafted and approved during my stay in the division after the merger of three banks.

1. **Policy for outsourcing of guards**. This policy aimed to outsource guards for bank requirements at any place. This policy was placed on board earlier in 2009, but the worker's director and officer director objected, and as such, it remained pending. The division with coordinating of HRD and security division had drafted a policy. However, the issue was that there should not be any industrial dispute when implementing the policy. The matter was also discussed with the workers' union, and their suggestions were considered. The policy was approved by the board and was circulated and implemented to the satisfaction of all. This policy was issued for the first time in the bank.

2. **Policy for preserving the bank's old records with outside agencies.** When the three banks were merged, PNB and OBC had already engaged agencies, but UBI had not engaged any agency. There were three agencies in the merged entity. The rates, terms, and conditions were different for all three. Now, the question was which agency should be allowed to shift old records. Therefore, the division had decided to stop shifting records by any agency till further orders and action were initiated to draft a policy for the merged entity. This policy was approved along with other operational guidelines. But it took 15 months. Later, the policy was part of the IAD policy for preserving old records.

3. The board also approved Expenditure power charts at all levels for different purposes for the merged entity.

The authorities were delighted with the division's performance, and one day, our MD said that the purpose of my promotion to CGM had been accomplished.

RETIREMENT AND AFTER

So, I retired from bank service after 38 years and seven months on 31st March 2022. During my career, I have received eight promotions from the clerical cadre to the Chief General Manager position. I got each promotion on the first chance, except on one occasion. For this beautiful journey, the credit goes to my parents, teachers, notably Sh Rawal Singh and his family, and my bosses from time to time, who recognized my hard work and helped me overcome the hardships I faced on numerous occasions. I also express my special thanks to my mother and father and wife, who stood by me every time and encouraged me to do the right things and stand by the truth.

After retirement, I am settled in my hometown, Bathinda, and have a busy schedule of 3/4 hours daily reading good books and newspapers plus two hours of healthy workout in the morning and evening. Constantly feeling busy and happy. THANKS GOD

Occasion of retirement

REVIEW OF BOOK "MY JOURNEY CART TO AEROPLANE"

In this book, Mr Mann has nicely explained, as to how with hard work, transparency, honesty and dedication, one can attain top positions, though starting the career from a humble beginning.

The author's experiences and lessons learned during course of his professional journey have been explained with clarity These are very valuable resources for any one aspiring to achieve success in the professional life.

I earnestly feel that this book is a must read for students, present bankers and other professionals.

– Gauri Shankar
(former Executive Director &
MD & CEO (addl. charge)
Punjab National Bank

In a world of banking where man eat men, achieving success is highly competitive. Today, large number of Gen X is opting for a career in banking but clueless how to perfect it. The autobiography of simple, novice and successful banker provides reading like a manual for achievers.

Entry to banking career, like Mr Mann, is not so common in today's context. However, the challenges he faced were big mountains at that time. It was the time when availability of information and communication were difficult tasks. With zeal towards improving the life, both personal and social, helped him to be a real banker. Book is full of examples of main traits needed for a successful banker, continuous learning and completing the task in time. There are lots of new learning and unlearning. With his simple approach towards giving his best has helped him rise to the highest ladder from clerk to become Chief General Manager in the bank is no ordinary feet and reading helps to understand how to climb step by step.

Every reader of the book will be greatly benefited by reading it provides.

– Gopal Singh Gusain
Member
Reserve Bank of India Services Board
Mumbai 21 June 2024

"My journey: Cart to Aeroplane" by Biker Singh Mann is an inspiring memoir that traces the author's journey from his humble beginnings in a small village to his successful career as a Chief General Manager at Punjab National Bank. The author's experiences and the lessons learned during his career are presented with clarity and honesty, making it a valuable resource for anyone aspiring to achieve success in their professional life. The author's experiences and the lessons learned during his career are presented with clarity and honesty, making it a valuable resource for anyone aspiring to achieve success in their professional life.

"My journey: Cart to Aeroplane" is more than just a memoir; it is a story of resilience, hard work, and the transformative power of education. The book is a testament to the power of hard work, determination, and the importance of education in transforming one's life. This book is a must-read for those seeking inspiration and practical advice on achieving success in any sphere of life through perseverance and integrity.

– Sh Sanjay Kumar
Executive Director (Retired)
Punjab National Bank

The simplicity with which Mr. Mann has shared the experience of a seasoned and practical banker who made his career path from grassroots to the top post in the hierarchy is praiseworthy. The patience and perseverance in dealing critical and challenging situations is definitely going to help young bankers aspiring a bright career in banking. Tips like confidence in self, a positive attitude, hard work, timely decision, relationship with colleagues etc. in dealing different situations are surely encouraging.

– Manas Ranjan Biswal
Executive Director (Retired)
Union Bank of India

The author's life story is a vivid illustration of how simple living and high thinking can guide one through the most challenging and rewarding paths. This book is an extension of his personality—honest, insightful, and profoundly motivational. It offers a rare glimpse into the experiences and wisdom of a man who has navigated the complex world of banking with grace and fortitude.

For readers, whether they are aspiring bankers, seasoned professionals, or individuals seeking inspiration, this book provides valuable lessons on the importance of perseverance, the power of humility, and the impact of leading by example. It is a guide to achieving professional success while staying true to one's values and principles.

– Rajiv Puri
EXECUTIVE DIRECTOR (Retired)
Central Bank of India

There is no dearth of books on bankers, it is very inspiring to read a story of a successful bankers with humble beginning. Mr. Mann has not only displayed insights into his journey but also challenges during his journey. The story of Cart to Aeroplane also displayed the role of Public Sector Bank in developing common person into a successful banker, which generally remain unnoticed by people. A must read for bankers, how continuous and steady efforts of a person made him realize his dreams and contribute to nations growth"

– Sh Vinod Kumar
Executive Director
Punjab National Bank

The experiences shared by Mr. Mann in his book "MY JOURNEY CART TO AEROPLANE" has shown his ability to create & understand the concept, and then to implement, made him a successful leader & a performer. His management rules used while working in bank and shared in the book will be definitely helpful for the next generation of bankers and students for all the success in career.

– Rajesh Verma
Chief General Manager (Retired)
Punjab National Bank

"My Journey – Cart to Aeroplane," is a collection of memoirs by Mr. B S Mann, retired as Chief General Manager from Punjab National Bank. His narrative traces his remarkable ascent from a humble beginning as a clerk to the prestigious position he held He candidly discusses the challenges he faced as a student and how he eventually pursued Commerce at Degree level without such background, achieving commendable scores through dedication and hard work His progression through different roles—from clerk, officer, manager, and Chief General Manager—exemplifies the practical application of organizational management theories. Whether transforming poorly performing branches or tackling problematic loans, or managing a Region or Zone. His methodical approach to problem-solving starting with defining the issues, analysing them, exploring alternatives, selecting viable solutions, and executing them with team support—is all portrayed vividly, akin to a compelling narrative. Though the memoir is written in a straightforward style, focusing more on substance than literary finesse, it captivated me with its insights and motivational content. I highly recommend this memoir as a source of inspiration and practical wisdom, particularly for those facing challenges in their banking careers.

– N. S. TOOR
(Mentor)
N S TOOR SCHOOL OF BANKING

The author who rose from the post of a junior bank employee to the top post of Senior General Manager in the bank due to his extraordinary qualities like hard work, dedication to the job, sincerity with department, determination to achieve, facing hard challenges with courage and confidence, professional competence and unimpeachable integrity. The book is an eye opener and meaningful lesson to be learnt for the new generations because it highlights the qualities which are helpful for them in achieving the highest goals in life. This is a rare example that the author who belongs to a family of a marginal farmer rural background with very less education facilities, has touched the highest peaks of success in his banking career. I convey my heartiest congratulations to Mr. Mann for making all out efforts in accomplishing this wonderful task by writing this inspiring text which must be a bonanza for the readers.

– Paramjit Singh Gill

IPS

Inspector General of Police Punjab (Retired)

Today I finished reading the book, "My journey, Cart to Aeroplane" by Shri Bikar Singh Mann. I know Mr. Mann since he was transferred to New Delhi as chief manager of a leading nationalized bank & have seen him achieving the status of an accomplished banker. Later, we were meeting OFF & ON during his Delhi visits but was always in touch without much business reason except as we share the similar roots. Whenever we met, I noticed a sense of achievement in him & his strong zeal to move ahead in his profession of banking was always evident. When sometimes, he narrated his work life I could see in him a successful implementer of ideas who means business. This book is epitome of that mindset. Apart from being a demanding boss, he also looked like easy to manage sub-ordinate & almost worshipped the assignments given by his bosses. Once he came to us in Gurgaon and both of us went to bless the daughter of one of his colleagues on her marriage. While having lunch, his colleague praised his banking knowledge & operational skills & told me, that Singh Sahib will surely achieve the position of a director before retiring. During our companionship, I saw him moving towards that position very fast. After his retirement as Chief General Manager, I came to know that he is writing his career path in the form of a book, I was so keen to read it as early as possible that I did not hesitate to request him to send me the manuscript itself, for which he kindly obliged. Apart from being a vivid reader, I wanted to know, why this journey got limited 'from cart to Aeroplane & does not end at corner office' of his bank.

Cart to Aeroplane is a very useful reference manual for a banker aspiring for operational excellence. Through small doses of anecdotes from his all postings in various positions, He has almost spoon fed the young executives that how the enablers are executed to achieve the desired results. Although he has explained all this as first person as a banker but we see the learnings which go into sub-conscious of the reader are applicable in any operations management situation. We learn how he developed & used his skills in customer satisfaction, human resource management, Conflict resolution, networking, planning & executing to say the least. Not shirking effort, we see, how beautifully he implemented the Japanese concept of GEMBA (Be at the place of action). As they say, the biggest qualification of a person is his courage & conviction & we read Mr. Mann showing that whenever & wherever the circumstances had put him into a difficult situation. Moreover he is seen deliberately working from domain of possibility & has exhibited his never say die attitude in his book.

I also commend his effort & really appreciate how he has kept himself topic focused while writing this book. While covering his four decade long worklife span, this is a great achievement indeed. The details in which he has mentioned the dates & numbers show his ever green dedication to his work while in any office & he has not forgotten his childhood in life & in the field of banking.

Apart from showing the way to young officers, he has created a legacy for the next generation in his family & we wish him all success in his coming literary creations. As he is planning to write part two of this book to make it a true biography, we look forward to know & learn more tactics of business & life from this friend of ours.

– Pavitar Singh
Vice President (Retd.)
Bharti Airtel Group

www.ingramcontent.com/pod-product-compliance
Lightning Source LLC
Chambersburg PA
CBHW031406150726
47989CB00002B/553